*She's counting the days until she can
let down her hair*

UNDISCLOSED

Elsa Miles

Published by Elsa Miles, Washington, DC

Publication Date: January 2020

Available in Ebook

Paperback ISBN: 978-1-7341782-1-0

Cover art by Elsa Miles via Canva

For those who like to cut straight to the spark, sizzle, and chase.

For those who like to cut straight to the spark, sizzle, and chase.

PROLOGUE

*R*oxanne Blair stopped short when she entered the office. What did HR and Legal want now?

"Ms. Blair, take a seat," said Melissa Bancroft, the personnel director.

Roxanne looked from Melissa to the company's attorney, Jim Doherty. "What's going on?" she asked.

"Take a seat," the attorney replied.

"I don't have time for this. I need to get back to Nick. We are swamped today." She hoped they wouldn't see through her bluff; she was busy, just not with Nick. For the past few days, he'd sent her to Accounting to work on a stupid, mind-numbing project—a space far from him. He'd been acting strange lately. Aloof and withdrawn. So what if she'd tried to kiss him? He'd been giving her the look for days. At least she thought he had been. She crossed her arms to stop herself from fidgeting like Julia Roberts in *Pretty Woman*.

She placed her hands on her hips and began to tap the toe of one of her red platform pumps. *Time's a-wastin', people.* The sooner she finished the project, the sooner she'd be back at her desk in the executive wing.

The attorney looked past her and nodded his head. A security guard entered with a box and set it on the desk before her.

Her purse strap hung from the corner of the box. "What are you doing with my purse?"

"Roxanne," the attorney spoke firmly, "please take a seat."

"I said I want to stand," she said and glared at the trio.

"As you wish." The attorney nodded at the personnel director. "Please proceed, Ms. Bancroft."

"Ms. Blair, here is a copy of your personnel file," Melissa said. "As you know, we have reprimanded you previously about sexual harassment in the workplace. The situation has worsened beyond repair, and we are terminating you."

"What? Are you insane?" She stormed closer to the attorney's desk. How dare Nick put her in this embarrassing position? He should have said something to her, and they could have settled this like adults. She'd show him. Tearing the file from Melissa's hand, she said, "You can't fire me! Nick Tremaine is harassing *me*! He's been propositioning *me*, you idiots!"

Jim stood. "Ms. Blair. You have been terminated and are no longer an employee of Tremaine Development. Our security officer will escort you from the property. Henceforth, if you step foot in these offices or go within one hundred yards of Nick Tremaine, you will be violating the restraining order we filed today."

CHAPTER 1

*L*ibby glided across the room with her MacBook Air and took the seat in front of the large executive desk. As usual, her boss had arrived earlier than everyone. "Good morning, Mr. Tremaine."

Nick lifted his head and regarded his ever-reliable assistant with curiosity. "You've been assisting me for eleven months now. You can call me Nick, you know." He grabbed a tie from his desk drawer and put it on, his stare never wavering.

"I'd rather not."

"Everyone else does."

"I'm not everyone else. I'm your assistant."

"That's the point," he countered. "Can you give me a good reason why we shouldn't be on a first-name basis when every other employee in this company is?"

She raised her blond brows behind her massive, thick-rimmed, non-prescription glasses. Libby could think of a perfect one: the distance it created. She could envision herself on stage at the company town hall addressing five hundred employees. *"Hi, I'm Libby Duncan. I've been pulling the wool over Nicholas Tremaine's eyes."*

Except now was not the time for confessions. Her boss wanted a good reason she wouldn't call him Nick, and she'd give him a safe, valid one.

"Professional boundaries," she said. "I heard through the grapevine that your last assistant crossed the boundaries of propriety between professionalism and … something else. I confirmed the rumors with Human Resources."

Nick kept his expression in check. He stared at her heart-shaped face framed by the large glasses and her seemingly ritualistic tight bun. One of the things he most liked about his assistant was how resourceful and inquisitive she could be. She seemed to know what was going on in every department and with every employee at all times. He should have known she'd learn about Roxanne Blair. His HR and Legal teams had advised him not to discuss the past incident with any employees, but he'd be damned before losing an excellent assistant to speculation. "Would you like to ask me anything about Roxanne Blair? Do you have any concerns about working with me?"

Libby shook her head. "None at all. If I did, I wouldn't still be here. Based on my experience with you, I would never believe you abused your authority in the company and certainly not with an employee. I told HR the same thing." *Besides,* she thought, *I know Roxanne all too well.* But she hoped he never found *that* fact out.

Nick didn't realize he'd tensed, worrying about her opinion, until he heard her words of faith and his shoulders relaxed. They worked well together, he respected her work ethic, and he was relieved she recognized his too.

"Thank you. I appreciate your trust and value your opinion."

"In that case, you should trust my judgment about using your surname." She looked over the rim of her glasses.

Direct as ever, he thought. "I appreciate your point. However, calling me Mr. Tremaine, when everyone else refers to me as Nick, doesn't fit with the company culture we are cultivating: a culture of peers, not hierarchy." He dropped his pen on his desk. "In a few months, most of our offices will be converted to an open-cubicle environment. We are taking great lengths to establish our corporate culture. The name is Nick; please use it."

"I will think about it," she said. *Darn it,* she thought. Calling him Mr. Tremaine offered distance and had allowed her to think of him more as an entity rather than a person—a person she was lying to, at least by omission.

Roxanne Blair had once been her stepsister. Libby's dad had married Roxanne's beauty pageant-loving mom when Libby was nine. The marriage hadn't lasted past five years, thank goodness; Libby had never been able to grow close to Roxanne or her mother, despite desperately wanting a sister and mother. And her dad had been miserable three out of the five years. Libby's mother had passed away during childbirth—Libby's birth. Now, the only connection Libby still had with Roxanne was Libby's self-appointed godmother, Grace. Grace was Roxanne's aunt, but Libby and Grace had formed a bond that Libby would always hold close to her heart and far away from her former stepsister.

Nick watched Libby's poker face. He could tell she was thinking deeply about something, but as ever, he couldn't guess her thoughts or emotions. On most days, that was fine with him, yet today he wished he had an inkling about what made his assistant tick. "Let's get to work," he said.

Libby was grateful he pulled her from the past and away from her guilt and deception. *It's temporary,* she reminded herself. *I won't mislead him forever.* "We need to go through your calendar for the next two weeks," she began. "There are several conflicts due to the conference next week."

"Speaking of which," Nick said as he turned the computer monitor so they could view his calendar together, "how is my PowerPoint presentation for the investor conference coming along?"

"It's almost done," Libby confirmed. "I'm still waiting for the Business Development team to provide their slides. Once they do, I'll consolidate the presentation for your review."

"Great. Pass it by Legal before you give it to me, please."

Libby typed a note on her laptop. "Will do. Ready to go through the calendar?"

"Ready."

As Libby leaned closer to the monitor, Nick's cologne wafted across the desk. *Very masculine, just like him,* she thought, suppressing a shiver of excitement. Roxanne had probably loved his cologne.

"Another damn busy week." He smiled as he scrolled through the schedule.

"You wouldn't have it any other way," she said.

He chuckled. "No, I wouldn't. And, I suspect, neither would you."

She couldn't help but smile. He was right. "A reporter from the *San Francisco Chronicle* called this morning requesting a conversation tonight. She wants an interview regarding the resort at Half Moon Bay."

"We can't disappoint the local press. Tell her I'll do it by phone after the planning development call at the end of the business day."

They finalized his schedule and then moved on to messages and emails requiring his attention. Libby took notes so she could respond to several on his behalf. After some time, she glanced at her watch. "It's time for you to join the conference call for the Compliance Committee."

Nick corrected the monitor and turned quickly in his chair. "I'll dial in now."

She gathered her things and headed toward the door.

"Thank you, Libby."

"Ms. Duncan," she corrected him without turning around. "But, you're welcome, Mr. Tremaine."

"So that's the way it's going to be?" he asked and laughed.

"For now. Until I'm comfortable," she said, which would be never if all went according to plan.

"For now, *Ms. Duncan.* For now."

She ignored the warning. "Do you want the door open or closed?"

"Open, please."

Libby slid behind her desk and began going through the interoffice mail. She listened to the deep, smooth tenor of Nick's voice. She glanced over her shoulder to look at him. His desk was in her direct line of sight. When she thought he might look up and catch her staring, she turned away. She enjoyed working for him even if she did her best to not outwardly show it with frequent smiles or comradeship.

What would he do if he knew I was a fraud? she wondered. Actually, she did know. He'd fire her. Technically, she wasn't doing anything wrong, and she hadn't lied on her application, but figuratively, she was lying to him every day. She wasn't proud of it either. But she was practical.

She frowned and looked across the room into the gold-framed mirror that was the size of her sliding glass door at home. It had been a bit unnerving when she first came to work to have her visage reflected across the room for an average of nine hours a day. Now, she looked at herself and her disguise: her long hair gathered in a tight bun, which was often the onset of a nagging headache by the end of the day, the sturdy glasses that were too large for her pale face, and the boring brown suit—one of many unflattering creations.

She smoothed her index finger over one temple and took a deep breath. She would love to let her hair down and apply some blush and mascara, maybe even some perfume to rival Nick's cologne. When the idea to interview for this job as a dowdy wallflower had taken shape, she hadn't fully appreciated the consequences and how deflating it would be to play down her looks and fashion sense. No one ever looked her way. She never caught anyone's eyes. She often felt invisible. *But it's all for a good reason,* she thought, trying to boost her morale.

Her phone rang, and she reached for it. "Nick Tremaine's office, may I help you?"

"Libby," Dana, her best friend and future business partner, squealed. "We got it!"

Libby stilled and stifled her hope until she was certain she understood. She looked in Nick's direction. He was in his own world. She dipped her chin to ask quietly, "We got it?"

"The bank just called. Our loan is approved."

Libby sank back against her chair. Finally. This loan put her one step closer to ending both her charade as Nick's assistant and her career as an assistant, period.

"Seconds Impressions is official," Dana said. "I can hardly believe it."

Their executive dating company was really going to happen. Libby straightened in her chair before someone could spot her in the non-Ms.-Duncan-like slouch. "As much as I wish I could, I can't talk here. I'll call you tonight after work." She rang off.

Out of their dateless desperation in San Francisco, she and Dana and had come up with the idea to start a dating service in the city that would allow groups of screened business professionals to spend 180 seconds on a first date. If both participants chose each other, they would be paired up via Seconds Impressions' website. All confidential. All secure.

Libby wanted to kick off her shoes, let down her hair, and dance around the office. Maybe do a few cheerleader jumps. Unfortunately, such a display of emotion would never suit her persona as an uptight professional assistant, so she settled for a mental happy dance.

She and Dana had spent weeks writing their business plan and identifying their target clients: business professionals, especially C-Level executives, both male and female. In the end, the business plan had been the easiest part. The most difficult step had been getting Libby in a position to be surrounded by their target audience of single professionals so that she could tap into their heads, work-life balance, and lifestyles to find out what they were looking for in a companion, and which dating process would best work with their hectic schedules. Her current position with Nicholas Tremaine had also allowed Libby to establish relationships with event coordinators at top-notch restaurants, five-star hotels, and meeting facilities. All of which she planned to leverage someday and never let her boss find out about until she was good and ready, well-established in her new career as a corporate matchmaker.

Libby's grin stretched across her face, and she wiggled in her seat, fighting to contain her excitement. She and Dana still had months of work ahead of them before the business would support them, but they were on their way. Libby heard a chuckle and swiveled in her chair to see Nick watching her from his desk, eyebrows raised, the phone resting between his head and shoulder as he watched her. Still too excited, she couldn't remove the smile from her face.

Nick spoke into the phone, "Sorry, everyone. No, John. I wasn't laughing at you. It was a good point."

Libby turned back to her computer and felt the flush rising up her neck and infusing her cheeks. *Dumb, Libby. Really dumb,* she thought. That was not Ms. Duncan behavior at all. She looked over her shoulder to see if he was still watching. Fortunately, he had refocused on his call. *Good.* She stared a little longer while she could.

He was gorgeous. Too gorgeous for his own good. Libby thought of her materialistic ex stepsister, Roxanne. It was not hard to imagine Roxanne harassing this man or trying to sink her manicured talons into his hunkiness—and probably his bank account too.

Libby didn't blame Roxanne for being attracted to him. She'd overheard more than one discussion in the company cafeteria between employees, both male and female, crushing hard on her boss. Libby released a heartfelt sigh and glanced at the larger-than-life mirror again. *Roxanne probably loved this mirror.* Roxanne was beautiful and could stare at herself all day. If Libby looked like Roxanne, she'd love the mirror too.

Libby turned first one cheek and then the other to the large mirror. She smoothed one hand over her hair. Her starched collar rubbed against her soft neck. She trailed a finger along her jaw and underneath the fabric.

"Penny for your thoughts?"

Libby jumped.

Nick stood in the doorway, pulling on his jacket and straightening his tie. She remained silent, embarrassed that he had caught her staring in the mirror while wishing she could dress normal.

"You're a tough one. How about a dollar for your thoughts?" he asked.

She shook her head.

He upped the ante. "Alright, but this is my final offer, *Ms. Duncan.* A buck fifty?"

She smiled, ignoring the slur of her name and improvised. "I was trying to think of a more appropriate location for the mirror."

He tilted his head and looked hard at her. "No. I doubt that was what you were thinking about."

She turned back to her desk and reached for his iPhone,

handing it to him when he stopped in front of her desk. "I downloaded the apps you requested and installed all the updates. Time to go. You'll be late."

He slid the phone inside his jacket pocket and then pulled two dollars out of his wallet, dropping the bills on her desk. He saluted her. "You owe me fifty cents. I'll see this afternoon."

After he left, Libby reached for her purse to head out for lunch with her godmother. Before she reached the door, she turned and walked across the room and into Nick's office. She scrounged in her purse and stacked two quarters on his desk. "Now we're even."

CHAPTER 2

*L*ibby all but skipped to the restaurant. She smoothed her hand over her hair and went inside, following the hostess to a table.

"Grace." Libby smiled and leaned over to kiss her godmother's cheek and then took a seat at the white linen-covered table. As Libby pulled off the heavy glasses and threw them in her purse, Grace slammed her pair on her nose.

Grace looked horrified as she looked over Libby, cringing over the brown suit. "Since when do you wear glasses? What in the world are you wearing? What is wrong with your face?" Grace leaned over to brush a thumb across Libby's cheek and frowned at the gray film left behind on her thumb. "If my sister could see you now, she'd roll over in her grave."

True, Libby thought. Her stepmother, Wanda, had always been appalled with Libby's looks no matter how she tried to copy Roxanne. "You're not pageant material like Roxanne," Wanda had always said.

"It's nice to see you too," Libby said.

"Of course it's nice to see me; I'm not dressed like a mortician's wife, but I can't say the same for you," Grace said. Her smoker's voice accentuated the word *mortician*.

"Come now. I'm not dressed like a mortician's wife," Libby said. "Surely morticians even look better than I do," she said, not joking.

"You're right. You look more like a dead woman. Start explaining," Grace said.

After the waiter took their order, Libby leaned toward her godmother. She'd managed to describe her job as simply an administrative post for the past months, and she'd never met Grace for lunch during a workday. This plain look definitely needed an explanation. "You're not going to like it."

Grace looked at Libby's tight bun and shapeless suit jacket. "I already don't."

"I took Roxanne's old job."

Grace coughed fitfully. She grabbed the glass of water Libby handed her and took a sip. Once she caught her breath, she said, "With news like that, you're going to kill me before Roxanne's escapades do."

"I couldn't help it, Grace. When you told me about Roxanne's old job and how much she was making, it was irresistible."

"And you decided to ignore the little part about Tremaine harassing her?" Grace asked.

Libby sat up and smoothed her napkin over her lap. She wasn't sure why, but she felt very defensive of Nick, and Grace's comment pricked her hide. "I can promise you he did not. It was the opposite."

"I need nicotine before I can hear the rest of this." Grace started to dig through her purse.

"Here, suck on this instead."

Grace's face puckered and swatted at Libby's hand. "You are out of your mind. Why would I suck on a lemon?"

Libby dropped the lemon in Grace's water glass instead.

Grace popped a piece of Nicorette gum into her mouth and leaned forward on the table. "Okay. Talk to me."

"I did hear everything you said, but Roxanne being Roxanne, I figured there was more to the story. I've been on the other end of her lies. And you know her too."

Grace nodded, chewing furiously. "Continue."

"I applied and was interviewed by the personnel director. Whether Roxanne was the harasser or the harassed, I figured that Personnel would want to hire a wallflower. An excellent and well-qualified assistant, but a wallflower or someone older."

"Someone who would never aim for her boss like Roxanne would." Grace caught on and tried to pop her gum and was disappointed when the chalk-like texture did nothing. She spit it into a tissue. "So, you came up with this outfit?"

"Yes. I didn't think they would call me back, but they did. I did my research. He wasn't harassing her. I started eleven months ago, and everything has been fine," Libby said.

"Eleven months ago! Are you're only telling me now? Roxanne said she had to get a restraining order," Grace said.

Libby patted Grace's weathered hand. "She doesn't have

the restraining order. Nick Tremaine has the restraining order against her."

"Are you absolutely sure, Libby?"

"Yes. I didn't want to have to do this, but ..." Libby reached into her purse and pulled out her iPhone. She tapped the screen a few times and turned it toward Grace. "This is a picture of Nick Tremaine."

Grace moved her glasses higher on her nose and frowned at the handsome man. She rolled her lips between her teeth. "You're right. Roxanne would have been on cloud nine if he harassed her. She was probably trying to lick him from head to toe."

"Exactly." Libby sat her iPhone on the table. "Please keep this between us."

Graced waved a hand at her. "Of course. But what did you do when he found out you know Roxanne?" Grace asked.

"He hasn't. It's been years. I hardly know her now ..." Libby began, but Grace gave her a stern look, and she blushed. "I will tell him at the right time, if I must. I can't imagine why it would be necessary." She leaned forward and smiled. "Dana and I got our loan. We're official."

"That's wonderful news," Grace said. She reached for Libby's phone and tapped the screen. She looked at the picture of Nick for a few seconds more and turned it back toward Libby. "But be careful, honey. He doesn't look like he suffers fools. I'd hate to see all of your hard work fall apart over this deception."

Deception. Yes, that's what is ... Libby took the phone and put it in her purse. "I know. But I'm doing a great, professional job for him. No one is being hurt, and he doesn't have a clue that I'm anything but a dowdy wallflower." And she hoped she could keep it that way.

CHAPTER 3

*L*ukas Cooper was distracted by the noise coming from the outer office. He heard his assistant's raised voice just before a beautiful brunette threw open his door and glided toward his desk.

"Mr. Cooper, I do not appreciate your wasting my time." Roxanne Blair glanced around his office with disdain and wrinkled her nose.

Luke nodded at his perturbed assistant as he closed the door, rolling his eyes as if to say, *I can't believe we have to work with this woman.*

Luke couldn't either. "Ms. Blair. Have a seat."

Roxanne took a tissue out of her purse and wiped off the seat of the chair. She seated herself and crossed her long legs. "A gentleman usually stands for a lady until she takes her seat, Mr. Cooper."

"Yes, well, we are missing *one* of those people, aren't we?" He leaned back in his chair and placed his hands behind his head and waited.

On the spot, Roxanne disliked his personality almost as much as she hated his choice in clothing. *Almost.* But her father had said he was the best. And she deserved the best. Cooper's obnoxious red and white Hawaiian-print shirt stretched tightly across his chest. Red was her favorite color, but how was this man a successful lawyer dressed like that? "Says the man who dresses as poorly as he decorates his office," she said and brushed a piece of lint from her otherwise immaculately tailored red suit. "You're like a rerun of that bad show, *Magnum P.I.*, but sans mustache and short shorts."

Luke chuckled and took in the beauty queen before him. On the outside, she was gorgeous: dressed sexy as hell and well put together. Not a hair was out of place, and her lipstick was perfectly applied to her thick lips. Too bad she was a money-hungry monster on the inside. She was a cliché, and Luke hated clichés. She ruined it for the more deserving, the honest.

"The office suits my needs, Ms. Blair. I do pro bono work. But you already know that, otherwise you wouldn't be sitting here."

She pouted her luscious lips.

Yes, she thought, *but I also know you're wealthy.* Her father had told her so, or rather, he'd told her Luke was wealthy because he never lost. "Let's get to the point, shall we, Mr. Cooper? When is my day in court with Nicholas Tremaine?"

Luke pulled her thick file out of his desk drawer and dropped it on his desk. "I'm not your first lawyer. You're more than familiar with the process, I'm sure. I've contacted your former employer to set up depositions.

Depending on the outcome of those depositions, we will motion for arbitration."

He counted to three in his head, and bingo, she brought on the drama.

"Arbitration?" Roxanne forced a tear and reached for her hanky to gently dab at the corners so as to not ruin her makeup. "Couldn't we skip the depositions and go straight to court? My nerves can't take it any more." She sniffled.

Nor could her bank account, Luke knew. He'd had a friend run a background check on her. He leaned back in his chair. The lady had ice running through her veins, and if she had balls, they'd be steel. "I'm sure your nerves can handle it a while longer." He had read the personnel files already supplied by Tremaine Development. She didn't have a chance in hell. The irritation rose swift and hard through his blood. *Damn favors*. If Roxanne Blair wasn't Roger Blair's daughter—estranged or otherwise—he wouldn't be in this position. How in the hell did this woman come from Roger's blood? His gut told him she was an egomaniac who was furious that Nicholas Tremaine had rejected her pursuit. She wanted revenge for being rejected, pure and simple. And there were victims out there, women who had been groped and abused, who truly needed his help.

He remembered when Roger entered his office just two weeks before and outlined the story of his daughter's dilemma.

"No way, Roger. *You* don't even believe her. And I'm trying to catch the bad guys, not the good ones."

"You owe me," Roger had said.

"Yeah, I owe you, but not at the risk of my reputation.

Call in your favor for a better purpose." Luke crossed his arms over his chest and met Roger's formidable stare.

"One case won't hurt your reputation. You own your career. And who cares? You're a millionaire."

"Yes, by taking cases I believe. This, Roger"—he shoved the file across the desk—"is a load of crap."

Roger had dropped his head. "Please, Lukas. You've got to help me. She is my only daughter, and this is all she talks about. I left my first wife when Roxy was a baby. Maybe if I'd been a better father, she'd be a better person. I'm trying to make things up to her. She needs your help. Make her see that it's pointless. Deep down, she's a good girl. Her mother just screwed her up with all of those damn pageants. She'll listen to you. Otherwise, she'll sign up with some vampire of a lawyer who will string her along, and I'll never hear the end of it. If she doesn't learn and change soon, when will she?"

Luke had wanted to say, *People don't change* and *She's your daughter, not mine,* but his older friend looked so exhausted that Luke instead frowned and threw his hands up. "She doesn't even know me."

"Everyone listens to you in the end, Luke," Roger said, his spirits lifting as if he knew Luke was bending. "Do this for me, and I'll never ask you for anything again."

"I don't like being ignored," Roxanne snapped, pulling Luke out of his memories.

"Yeah, I heard you. But we are starting with depositions." He leaned forward and stared her hard in the eyes.

She didn't flinch.

Roxanne never backed down, and he could at least like

21

that about her. "On your way out, ask James to set up a time for you to come in on Monday to do *your* deposition. And apologize to him while you're at it. If you were once a good assistant, then you should know that assistants are the real people in charge. Don't take advantage of his diplomacy." He turned back to his work, dismissing her.

She stiffened. She took her time standing and made a great show of brushing invisible dirt from her skirt. "Filthy." She wrinkled her nose again.

Alas, he liked it when she did that nose bit. She reminded him of Samantha on *Bewitched*. He'd watched reruns growing up and had always had a crush on the witch.

Roxanne looked down said button nose at him. "Mr. Cooper, I don't like you."

"That's okay, *sweetheart*. The feeling is mutual."

Roxanne was relieved she made it to her car before she let the angry tears flow. Others would call it a tantrum, she knew, but she was so fed up with having to put on a show constantly. What type of damn attorney was stupid enough to call a client suing for sexual harassment, "sweetheart"? So far, he seemed to go out of his way to push her buttons. She knew he was mocking her. Even if her father, who had been mostly absentee, had pulled a few strings, she knew Lukas Cooper wouldn't even be talking to her if she didn't look the way she did. Then again, she wouldn't be in trouble if she didn't look the way she did. Yes, she had hit on Nick, but hadn't he encouraged her? Yes, he had. She was sure she hadn't imagined the chemistry. She turned on the air conditioning and tilted the vents toward her face to dry her tears.

Mama had taught her that life is a performance and that she should always put on her best face; otherwise she'd never win. "Losing is for crybabies," her mom had always said. Roxanne was going to win this time.

CHAPTER 4

*L*ibby returned from lunch and sat down to screen her and Nick's emails. She froze when she saw the email from Lukas Cooper, Attorney at Law. The subject read: *Roxanne Blair*. She opened the email with dread.

Roxanne had found an attorney to take her case after eleven months of attorneys saying she didn't have a case. *Ugh.* So much for going the next few months and getting out of this job without any more mentions of her former stepsister.

She dialed Melissa Bancroft's extension in Human Resources and told her the bad news.

"Shoot," Melissa said. "Doesn't she know when to quit? She's wasting everyone's time and giving women a bad reputation."

Feeling guilty, Libby remained silent.

"Add me to Nick's calendar today if you can squeeze me in, so that we can discuss our next steps. Can you forward me the email? Copy Legal, too, please." Melissa rang off.

Libby reread the email and looked up Lukas Cooper

online. A few headlines and links stood out: *The Can't-Lose Attorney*; *Attorney Donates A Half Million to Local Schools*; *Single Attorney with Scruples Most Eligible Bachelor*.

Libby exited the search. Scruples? Why would anyone with scruples take Roxanne's case? She printed out a copy of the email and set it on Nick's desk.

Melissa was right. Roxanne didn't know when to leave things alone. Libby had attended enough of Roxanne's childhood pageants to realize she was a sore loser. One time, Wanda and Roxanne had invited her backstage at a pageant. A sweet redhead with a gift for baton twirling was sure to win. Libby had watched, horrified, as Roxanne hid the girl's baton. With no backup, the girl had withdrawn. Roxanne had won that show. Libby never went backstage again. When she could get out of it, she avoided the pageants altogether.

She wondered how Nick would react to this latest development. Since he was the one in the right, she believed he had nothing to worry about, and this was more of a nuisance than anything else. She hoped she was right.

Libby didn't have long to wait.

Nick smiled at her when he returned. He took off his suit jacket as he walked toward his office and hung it over the back of his chair. He leaned over and slid his index finger along the print-out on his desk. He briefly tensed and then tossed the page in his recycle bin. He picked up the two quarters sitting next to his laptop, one corner of his lips tilted as he caught her eye across the room. He sat down and activated his computer, rolling one of the quarters back and forth between his fingers, along his knuckles like a magician.

Relieved that the email from Cooper didn't seem to upset him, Libby returned to her work. If Nick wasn't worried about Roxanne, then Libby wouldn't worry about him. Perhaps nothing more would come of this. Besides, she had a lot of work to do before she could go home and work on Seconds Impressions.

Nick cocked his head to hold the phone in place as Libby entered his office with paperwork to sign. After scrawling his bold signature and looking up at her, he extended the documents toward her with a half smile.

But he didn't release the papers immediately. Holding on to the other end of the files, his assistant raised her eyebrows in silent inquiry.

He reached with his free hand to hit the mute button. "I'm leaving after this call. Don't wait for me."

"Perfect," she said. "Goodnight."

He released the papers and pushed the mute button on the phone to resume the conversation.

Nick waited to hear the outer door open and close, signaling *Ms. Duncan's* departure. He glanced at his watch.

Four minutes after five p.m. He would typically work for another two hours, but he couldn't wait for this call and day to end. He'd talk to the reporter from home. *Damn Roxanne Blair.* She was like a post-apocalyptic zombie in one of his author-aunt's books; no matter what he did, she just kept coming back for more.

He interrupted the client to correct an error in the building proposal. He sat back while the conversation continued, offering his opinion when needed as the partners and founder of one of his top clients argued the finer points.

Ten after five. *Time is dragging, kind of like this discussion.*

Nick swiveled in his chair to stare out his fourth-story office window. He was usually too distracted to take advantage of the view. He remembered when he first got the office space several years before how much he'd liked to watch people scurrying about like ants, anxious to get home, while he'd always felt a sense of well-being remaining behind to pursue his passion in work. With his heels, he scooted his chair on wheels closer to the window so he could look down at the rush-hour crowd. To his surprise, he immediately recognized his assistant's blond bun bobbing below.

Libby strolled into his view to stand in line for the express commuter bus. He chuckled at a joke made by a partner but didn't move his attention from his assistant. He wondered what she was like in her personal life. Did she wear that ridiculously tight bun and the large glasses all night long?

He stood gingerly and leaned his shoulder against the window, curious to see if she would keep to herself or if she would speak to the people in line with her. Would she shed any of her daily formalities? He didn't have long to wait.

His assistant dropped her bag between her ankles, and to his complete surprise, yanked the pins from her constrictive bun. With wide eyes, he watched her run eager fingers through her gloriously long, finally unbound blond hair. He could almost feel her slender fingers gliding across her tender scalp, massaging away its daylong abuse. She tilted her head back and looked up to the sky and smiled while she was at it. He caught his breath, surprised by his body's immediate response.

The older man standing in front of her must have said something funny because she flashed him a gigantic smile and tossed her head back in laughter.

Nick wished he could see her eyes past those large hideous eyeglasses. Surprising himself, he realized he'd like to hear her laughter too. His traitorous dick stiffened further. Shocked by his reaction, he shook his head. What was wrong with him? If Roxanne Blair could see him now … He glanced at his watch. Surely Libby's bus should arrive soon, and he could shed this ridiculous, and hopefully momentary, interest. But until then, he would keep watching, his conference call forgotten.

When the bus pulled up, she practically skipped up the stairs. Not only did she shed the bun each evening, but she also seemed to shed five years. The doors closed, and he returned to his chair and conference call. He glanced at his watch again: twelve minutes after five. He knew already that he'd be watching the clock tomorrow to see if this was a daily event. The show was over, but his smile stuck around for the duration of his teleconference. Libby Duncan had proven herself to be a professional and competent assistant. He might not understand why she dressed the way she did at work, but she wasn't hurting anything or anyone as far as he could tell. Now, he needed to convince his hormones to cooperate in the future. He'd never reacted to someone he worked with before, regardless of Roxanne's claims.

~

Libby grabbed one of the last available seats on the bus. She removed the heavy glasses and tossed them in her bag. With her index finger and thumb, she rubbed the bridge of her nose. When this was all over, she hoped she wouldn't have permanent pockets. She wondered if anyone, aka Nick, would notice if she switched to a smaller, less burdensome pair. Surely she was enough of a wallflower these days that she could manage a small change unnoticed. She couldn't imagine wearing those huge glasses for another year until Seconds Impressions was on its feet.

Within twenty minutes, she reached her stop, exited the city bus, and walked the last block to her loft rental apartment. She smiled as always as she made her way down the sidewalk. She had moved here shortly after she went to work for Nick.

Libby threw her keys on the table as she walked from the foyer through her bright living room, and then upstairs to her bedroom. She methodically removed her brown, straight-cut jacket, her boring brown skirt, and notice-me-not white blouse and proceeded to hang the shapeless suit on the right side of her closet next to the equally dull blue, gray, and black suits. She kicked off the comfortable wide-toed pumps with square heels that would make a podiatrist proud, stripped off the restricting nude nylons, and wiggled her toes. Her toenail polished matched her pink bra and underwear. She used her hip to slide the closet door to the right.

She loved this part of her day and smiled as the left side of the closet materialized. She grabbed a floral tank top and yoga pants. Dressed as she should be, Libby trailed through her home until she reached the sunroom, which she had converted to an office. Switching on some music, Libby settled at her computer and waited while it came to life.

She reached for the business plan and called Dana.

"Hello?" Dana answered.

"Hello, partner."

CHAPTER 5

*L*ibby wasn't surprised to find Nick engrossed in his work when she arrived the next morning. Seven-thirty a.m. and from the looks of it, he'd been at work for some time. She turned on her computer and walked quietly into his office.

"Good morning, Mr. Tremaine."

"It's Nick."

He glanced her way but didn't quickly return to his work like normal. Was it her imagination or was he looking at her funny? She was about to ask him if she had something on her face, but just then he returned to the blueprints spread across his desk, leaning forward to squint at them.

Libby walked over to the east window and turned the blinds slightly, just enough to cut the morning sun's glare splashing the side of his face.

"Better?" she asked.

"Thank you. I hadn't noticed."

She acknowledged his gratitude with a slight nod and walked away.

Nick stopped working long enough to watch her cross the room.

He'd dreamt about her last night. It had been innocent enough, but he'd found himself more excited than usual to get to the office today, as if she would have ditched the bun or something. But alas, her tight bun was back.

But she did have an extra bounce to her step this morning, similar to the energy he'd witnessed last night when she hopped on her bus. His eyes paved a trail from her nondescript shoes to her trim ankles, nice-looking calves, and up to her backside—a pointless endeavor considering her long shapeless jacket covering it. He shook his head. Why was he trying to look at her ass? He needed to get a grip. Maybe he was working too hard. Perhaps he needed some female companionship. A proper shag, as his British friend, Connor, would say. Only Connor with his British accent could get away with saying anything of the like in America and not sound like a complete asshole.

Libby stopped when she reached the door and turned. "Ben Johnston and Will Bradley from Sales will be here at nine a.m. You're free until then."

"Good," he affirmed as he returned to his work, reprimanding himself for ogling his assistant, grateful she showed no sign of catching his wayward glance. Just because he knew she transformed at the end of the day, he didn't need to act like a curious teenage boy or an unprofessional prick. "Please remind them and tell them to be on time. Ben is always late, and it's getting old."

"Of course."

"And Ms. Duncan?"

"Yes?"

"The name is Nick."

"Good morning, Libby. Is his majesty available?"

Libby waved Will Bradley into Nick's office. "*Mr. Tremaine* is expecting you."

"Is Ben here yet?" Will followed his question with a thorough perusal of her face and hair. As usual, he frowned —in disapproval, she supposed. Not that she cared what Will Bradley thought of her get-up.

"Not quite."

When he rolled his eyes, she smiled and said, "I called him. He said he wouldn't be late."

He turned to the office. "Good morning, Nick." Will took a seat across from his boss. He glanced around a minute later when he heard voices, relieved to see that his direct report had arrived and was now chatting with Nick's assistant. Why Ben liked talking to her, Will had no idea. The woman dressed like an old lady. Not Will's type at all. He looked back at Nick. "We have great news from the Sales department."

Nick closed his email and swiveled in his chair to face his Vice President of Sales. "Music to my ears." He glanced at his watch. "Where's Ben? We need to get started."

"Right now, he's flirting with your assistant."

Nick chuckled dismissively, disbelieving a word of it. When Will's expression remained serious, Nick raised one eyebrow and leaned to the right to peer out his doorway.

~

"Good morning, Libby," Ben winked at her. "You looked as dressed-down as usual."

"Be quiet; someone might hear you," Libby admonished, but then smiled. She ducked away as he playfully reached for the collar of her jacket. He was the only employee who truly knew her after running into her in her neighborhood market one weekend. After-hours Libby looked little like the Ms. Duncan most knew. But he'd kept her secret, was easy-going, and kind. And she liked him. It didn't hurt that he had blond hair, blue eyes, and to-die-for dimples. Though he wasn't her type, she hoped he would be one of their first customers at Seconds Impressions.

His voice was laced with sarcasm. "This gray makes you look pale and ill, and your hair …" He heaved a dramatic, forlorn sigh. "It makes you look as uptight as ever."

"Thank you," she said. "You better hurry."

He reached for her glasses, and she smacked at his hand. She giggled as he leaned across her desk to whisper, "Next Halloween, promise me it will be the one day that you don't wear this costume."

"Ben! You're late!" Nick shouted across his office.

"I'll call you later, Libby," Ben said, his voice raised a notch, while he swaggered into Nick's office to grab the vacant seat. Seemingly unperturbed, he missed Nick's expression.

Nick continued to stare at his assistant perched primly behind her desk. Was he mistaken, or did Ben call his assistant by her first name? And had he said he'd call her later? He wished he could have heard their preceding conversation.

"Johnston," Will laughed good-naturedly and shook his head from side to side. "When are you going to give up on Libby?"

Bradley too? Nick looked blankly from one man to the next. Was Nick the only one not allowed to call *his* assistant by her first name? Another contradictory and mysterious discovery.

"Never. Someday she'll take me up on my offer, and what a great day it will be." He patted the area over his heart.

Will rolled his eyes and continued to shake his head. He caught Nick's expression at the same time. "Sorry, Nick. We obviously got sidetracked."

"With my assistant?" Nick double-checked. He glanced again at his quiet, capable assistant. Her hair was still wound in a tight bun, not flowing down her slim back as he now knew it could.

"I know," Will assured him. "I don't see it either, but Johnston has it bad."

Ben pulled out his notes and smiled smugly at Nick and Will. *Too smugly*, Nick thought.

Ben said, "Gentlemen, with all due respect, let's just say everything is not as it appears. Never judge a book by its cover."

Although the two men became silent, Nick continued to regard his assistant through the doorway.

She must have felt the weight of his stare, for she glanced up. She raised her brows in silent question, and he thought her cheeks might be rosier than usual, but he'd have to be closer to confirm. He nodded toward the door. She rose gracefully and pulled the door shut. Had she always moved so elegantly? He shook his head to clear his thoughts. *Get it together, Nick.*

Nick faced the two men with a stern look.

Ben began to fidget under Nick's unwavering regard.

After a few minutes, Nick broke his silence. "When we finish here, I suggest the two of you stop by Personnel and review the company policy on sexual harassment."

Will looked surprised while Ben cringed. "Sorry, guys," Ben said.

"Now let's get started."

CHAPTER 6

*L*ibby's hands stilled on her keyboard, and she stared with confusion across Nick's desk. "Excuse me?" When he didn't answer, she glanced at the flat screen to reread the last line she'd typed. Yes, there it was, right in the middle of a letter to Mr. Krancoise regarding the beachfront development in Carmel: *Has Ben Johnston been harassing you or bothering you in any way?*

She was incredulous. "What?"

If it weren't such a serious issue, Nick would have smiled at her apparent surprise. Strangely, he found her disbelief charming. "Has Ben Johnston been harassing you or bothering you in any way?"

Her mouth opened and closed and opened and closed. "Of course not. Ben and I are friends. He lives in my neighborhood. He's completely harmless." Libby couldn't believe she was having this discussion. Truth be told, she felt extremely uncomfortable. She and Nick only ever had work-related discussions. And while this was technically work-related, it seemed infinitely more personal, and he seemed genuinely concerned—probably because of the Roxanne debacle.

Nick couldn't believe what he'd just heard. *Ben.* She'd referred to Johnston as Ben. Not Mr. Johnston. "Are you sure everything is okay? Based on my own experience, I won't tolerate sexual harassment in the workplace." Nick continued to stare across the desk at her, trying to read her eyes behind her thick-rimmed glasses.

Libby blushed, uncertain why she felt self-conscious. He was asking a simple question, after all. "Ben is a friend. You have nothing to worry about."

Ben again. But with the issue addressed as much as it could be for now, Nick nodded his head and let it go. "If anything changes with *Ben* or anyone else, I trust you will tell me? I won't tolerate anyone mistreating you."

Was Libby losing her mind, or was her boss now the one turning red?

"Of course," she said, her voice scratchier than usual. Later, when Libby had settled into her work with Nick, the absurdity hit her, and she was hard-pressed to stifle a giggle. *Oh, the irony*, she thought. She, Libby Duncan, the purposely plain-looking, drab assistant of Nick Tremaine actually had this discussion. As Nick continued his dictation, she bit her lip to distract herself from the laughter that was bubbling inside her, slowly making its way up her chest and finally, unfortunately, coming out as an unladylike snort.

She surprised even herself and would have been embarrassed if not for Nick's priceless expression. He was looking at her as if she had eight eyes. Her laughter came tumbling out. Tears of hysteria came next, and between gasps, she waved her hand at him to reassure him. "I'm sorry, I don't know what came over me." She took a deep breath and let it out on a sigh.

After another deep breath, she accepted the tissue he offered and took her glasses off only long enough to dash at the dampness pooling under her eyelashes. Thank goodness she didn't wear eye makeup to work. She straightened her shoulders, patted her warm cheeks with her hands. "Alright. Sorry about that. I'm ready to continue." She stared fixedly at the laptop, afraid she would fall into a second round of giggles if she made eye contact. She bit her lip.

Speechless, Nick stared at his assistant's flushed cheeks. Libby, his unflappable assistant, was full of surprises lately. He stared at her bent head. At least he didn't have to worry about losing his assistant due to harassment. The suggestion about Ben Johnston's interest had sent her into fits of laughter. Perhaps it was best that she didn't realize Ben was truly interested in her.

"Then let's get back to work."

Melissa Bancroft from Human Resources and Jim Doherty, Corporate Counsel, entered Nick's office and took a seat at his desk.

Nick sighed as he focused on them. "It's never a good sign when the two of you are on my calendar."

Melissa slid a copy of the letter toward him. "Roxanne Blair has a new attorney."

Nick didn't even glance at it. "Ms. Duncan already gave me a copy. So, what are our options?"

"She's suing for sexual harassment," Jim said, leaning forward and flipping to page three of the document. "We can offer a monetary settlement. That will keep the case out of court and the newspapers."

"Negative," Nick snarled. "She harassed me, not the other way around."

"We can settle at lost wages," Melissa offered. "Roxanne's goal has always been mercenary, I think."

"Or"—Jim sat back—"we can refuse the settlement and let them file suit. If they even will."

"What do you know about her attorney?" Nick pulled the email out of his recycle bin and scanned it. "Cooper?" Nick asked. The name rang a bell, and Nick hoped it wasn't the same Lukas Cooper whose name was in the news from time to time for good deeds. The Bay Area loved him.

"It's Lukas Cooper. He does mostly pro bono work now, and he never loses a case. But he also is reputed only to take a case if he believes in it. I know that she spoke with several other attorneys, and they refused."

Shit, it was the same Lukas Cooper. Nick was furious. "I'll be damned if I'm going to pay a penny to Roxanne Blair. I should be suing her."

"That's one of our options," Melissa said. "We have plenty of witnesses that you were her victim and not the other way around. The restraining order and her exit interview will both come out in a case, right, Jim?"

Jim nodded. "It's not a bad idea. We can counter-sue. Listen, Nick. Let's refuse the settlement. At most, it will go through arbitration—it will never go to court—and the truth will surface during the depositions, and the arbitrator will probably throw out her case. Sure, her attorney will want to do interviews and depositions. If Cooper's reputation is correct and he only stands for those he believes in, he'll probably drop the case after he hears from the witnesses."

Nick stared silently at his personnel director and lawyer. He reached over and grabbed his phone and buzzed Libby's desk. When she answered, he said, "Ms. Duncan, please set up a meeting with the Public Relations team for tomorrow." He'd prepare the team for potential negative press. If Roxanne could fool an attorney like Lukas Cooper, she could fool a journalist looking for a lead. He hung up. He nodded his head toward Jim Doherty and Melissa Bancroft. "Refuse the settlement. And it's not just about me." His blood boiled whenever he thought about the onslaught of groping and harassment charges that had hit the news of late, perpetrated by high-profile men in positions of authority. *Assholes.* "There are too many women out there who are true victims, and I refuse to let Roxanne muddy the waters for them."

CHAPTER 7

*N*ick had been distracted ever since his appointment with Melissa and Jim, and Libby felt terrible for him. She knew it must be frustrating to have worked as long and hard as he had over the past several years only to have the likes of Roxanne compromise his efforts. She hoped she never accidentally ran into her former stepsister; she might strangle her.

"Mr. Tremaine." Libby entered his office.

Nick swiveled in his chair, away from the window, a frown firmly etched on his face. He planted his palms on his desk in a demonstration of attempted focus. "I know, I'm behind schedule. No time to stare out the window and contemplate life."

"Actually," she said in a gentler voice than he was used to hearing from her, "your next appointment was rescheduled, so you have an hour to get some work done. I'm running out for lunch. Can I bring anything back for you?"

Nick stared hard at his assistant. "Are you feeling sorry

for me?" His eyes might be playing tricks on him, but he could swear a little color climbed her neck to peek above her stiff white collar.

She lifted her chin and rolled her shoulders back. "Absolutely not," she said, returning to her usual sensible tone. "Why would anyone feel sorry for you?"

"Because of Roxanne Blair and her new attorney." Despite his sour mood, he felt a smile teasing the corner of his lips.

"Well, there is that," she quipped. "But no, I was only offering to bring back lunch because you get rather rude when you get hungry. Hangry, I think it's called. Self-preservation."

He chuckled. So his assistant had a sense of humor. For a brief second, he recalled Ben Johnston's flirtation and wondered what they'd said to one another. "Hangry? We can't have that"—he stood and grabbed his suit jacket—"I'll go with you."

Libby froze. "I was offering to *bring* your lunch. You should try to catch up with work."

Ah-ha. She didn't want him to tag along. He slid his jacket on and reached over to lock his computer. He glanced briefly at her. "Were you planning on meeting someone else?" *Maybe, Ben Johnston?* he wondered.

"No," Libby said, frowning. "But—"

"Did you want some time alone?" he asked.

"No …"

"In that case, lunch is on me. I could use a walk."

They were quiet in the elevator, and despite the beautiful sunny day, Libby frowned as they walked in silence.

"Why the frown?" Nick asked. Perhaps he'd been rude to foist himself on his assistant. As he stared down at her delicate profile, he told himself he should feel guilty about usurping her time alone, and yet, he didn't.

Libby shook herself. She could be honest and admit it felt strange to spend time with Nick outside the office, but she couldn't admit she looked forward to taking off the two-ton eyeglasses during her lunch hour and giving the bridge of her nose a break. She could only imagine how sore her head would be by the end of the day.

"I don't want to eat anywhere nice," she said instead. "I would rather grab a sandwich and spend some time outside. Sunlight. It's good for our circadian rhythms." A sit-down lunch would take far too long. What would they talk about?

Circadian rhythms? "Sounds good." Nick took her to an outdoor café. "Will this do?"

She nodded.

They ordered their sandwiches at the counter, and Nick carried their trays outside. The tables with umbrellas were taken. The unusually warm weather was not the norm for San Francisco. Nick peered at the sky and then at her pale skin before setting their lunches down. "Despite your circadian goals, I hope you brought some sunglasses." And sunscreen, he was tempted to add.

She sighed inwardly. Of course she had brought sunglasses, but unfortunately, she wouldn't be able to replace her costume glasses and wear them; they were highly fashionable, and not at all Ms. Duncan-like. She took her seat and squinted at him as he handed her lunch to her.

"Thank you."

He put on his sunglasses. "You're welcome." He paused before he took a bite. "You really don't have sunglasses with you?"

She improvised. "Unfortunately, they are nonprescription." If she could pat herself on the back for the quick excuse, she would.

He winked. "Go for it. I won't ask you to read anything."

She'd look like an idiot to refuse. Perhaps even suspicious. Her eyes were beginning to water at the brightness. She grabbed her purse and turned away from him.

Nick watched his assistant. He couldn't quite figure her out. She was always straightforward and never shy. But right now, she seemed uncomfortable, which he didn't mean to be a part of—he was only suggesting she wear sunglasses. Add to this the fact that she transformed at the bus line, well, go figure, but his assistant was becoming quite mysterious. When she turned back, Nick was surprised to see that she had much better taste in sunglasses than in her entire wardrobe. The smaller glasses framed her face well, emphasizing her cheekbones and making her lips look fuller. But, crap, why was he looking at her lips? Thankfully, his sunglasses hid the direction of his glance. After his meeting earlier about Roxanne Blair, he should be cautious.

They ate in companionable silence. It didn't take Libby long to find a second benefit to her sunglasses: she could stare at her boss as much she wanted. He was in deep thought. And while she ate her lunch, she allowed herself the guilty pleasure of watching his face. After all, he had great lips.

"Ms. Duncan?" Nick asked.

"Yes?" She dropped her eyes from his lips to his jaw. *Strong jawline, too,* she thought.

"You haven't said anything about Roxanne Blair's latest efforts."

She paused with a pickle halfway to her mouth. "Other than making sure the appropriate meetings are on your calendar regarding it, it's none of my business." She bit squarely into the pickle.

Unintentionally, Nick's eyes followed the action. "None of your business? You're my assistant, and the previous one is claiming I created a hostile work environment." He watched as she took a second bite of her pickle and licked some juice from her bottom lip. Damn, but he had never noticed that Ms. Duncan even had lips. Maybe he did prefer her overly clunky glasses. He sat back in his chair and crossed his legs and arms.

She faced him head-on and leaned to one side of her chair and crossed her legs too. "As I told you the other day, I've worked with you long enough to know better. I don't believe her." Now was *not* the time to tell him she knew Roxanne.

"What if you're wrong?" Absurd, but he was challenging her.

"Am I?" An arched brow peeked above the rim of her dark glasses.

"No," he confirmed. "You're not. I promise that I never harassed her."

"That's what I thought." She flashed him a saucy grin.

"I'm never wrong." Libby was definitely behaving wrong right now, she didn't know what had gotten into her, but she was never wearing sunglasses around her boss again.

He chuckled and reached for her tray. "Let's head back to work." He wasn't sure why it mattered to him so much that his assistant trusted him, but it did.

Back at their building, she turned to him when they reached the elevator to their offices. "Have you decided about the New Entrepreneur Gala next week?" Libby was desperate for him to decline the event so that she could go with Dana as the newfound owners of Seconds Impressions. If he went, Dana would have to go on her own. Libby couldn't risk Nick seeing the real her.

"Depends what's going on with the Roxanne Blair thing by then. If it's behind us, I'll go. If not, I'll probably avoid it. Puts me in a bad mood, and that's not the attitude I need to bring to an event intended to congratulate new business owners."

Damn you, Roxanne, Libby thought.

CHAPTER 8

A week later, Libby desperately wanted to flick a paperclip at her boss and hit him in the center of his forehead. Maybe then he would quit quizzically staring at her, something he'd been doing more and more. She racked her brain to think of something she may have said or done out of character. His puzzling looks were unnerving, like he was on to her secrets.

Plus, she needed a decision about the New Entrepreneur Gala. Since the depositions were scheduled for next week, she hoped Nick would decline, which meant Libby could attend with Dana. Yet, he was still non-committal.

Upon his arrival a few minutes after hers, he had summoned her to his office. She'd promptly taken her seat across from him, ready to jump into the day's work. That was a minute ago. As of yet, he had not said a word and only looked at her. Her patience was wearing thin, and as a result, a headache was coming on. She rubbed a temple.

"If it bothers you so much, why wear it so tight?" His

eyes drifted from the frown between her brows to her constrictive bun and then her temple-rubbing fingers. "You obviously have a headache."

"It's not my hair that's bothering me," she mumbled.

The implication didn't escape him, but he was annoyed with her too. Blame the state of his mood on Roxanne Blair and the upcoming deposition with Lukas Cooper, or blame it on his assistant's metamorphosis at the end of each business day, what did it matter? For a week now, he'd turned to his window after work hours to watch his assistant go through the same transition each day: hair down, eager fingers combing through her roots. Why did she persist on wearing the stupid bun?

Yet, was it any of his business? No, it wasn't. He bent to his work, embarrassed.

After a few instructions, she gratefully gathered her things to exit. At the door, she turned to him, fingers mentally crossed. "Have you decided yet if you will attend the New Entrepreneur Gala tonight? I need to RSVP for you. It's late."

He shook his head. "Highly doubt it. I'd rather work tonight, and I'm not feeling social. I'll see if my friend Connor wants to go instead. Leave the invite with me."

It took everything Libby had to hide her excitement. This night meant everything to her and Dana as new entrepreneurs. While she'd spoken to Connor O'Neil often on the phone, she'd only met him once in person, and only briefly. There was no concern he'd recognize her at the event. Now, she could let her hair down, so to speak, and openly mingle and network for Seconds Impressions. Sure, even without Nick attending, Libby would need to be on the lookout for people she knew through work—after all, she would dress as the real Elizabeth Duncan, not Nick's reliable assistant—and she didn't want to raise the alarm.

"Ms. Duncan," Nick asked, bemused by his assistant's lost thoughts. "Was there anything else?"

Libby shook her head. For a brief moment, she wished she could be honest about her long-term goals. But then she'd also have to be frank about Roxanne, and that would mean losing her job. "No. Nothing else."

CHAPTER 9

$\mathcal{D}$ana stiffened and stared over Libby's shoulder. "He's here and headed this way. I thought you said he wasn't coming," Dana hissed.

"He *wasn't*," Libby said, gulping. *Blast it. What are you doing here, Nick?* "Is he coming toward me?" Libby croaked and barely stopped herself from turning around to look for him. "What should I do?"

"We've got to get you out of here. Or, what if we stay and say you're with me, like we planned if you ran into anyone you did know from work?"

Libby's panicked eyes darted to the veranda doors next to her. "Looking like this?" Libby indicated her cocktail dress, hair, and makeup.

"Yeah, good point. He'd fire you for sure."

Libby's pulse quickened as her nerves frayed. "I'll go outside and hide on the balcony. Let me know when he's gone, and then we can leave. Or I can leave, and you can stay. And for heaven sake, keep Roxanne away from me."

That had been the other annoying development. Her

ex-stepsister had shown up, who knew why or how; Roxanne was far from an entrepreneur. Maybe she was with her next victim.

"Okay, he's still headed this way, but he isn't looking at you. I don't think. If anything, he looks hunted. Go. Now."

Nick had probably seen Roxanne, Libby guessed. Libby forced a polite smile at the group next to her and slipped outside. Skirting the light spilling through the floor-to-ceiling French doors, she retreated to the darkest corner and leaned against the rail. He'd never spot her here. Finally, she could breathe.

Waiting for her heart to return to a normal rhythm, she stared up at the starlit sky. That had been too close. She hugged herself to ward off the cool Bay breeze. Her strapless gown was classy and professional but not practical for the oceanside weather. She hoped Dana would figure out something soon.

Instead, she heard Dana's voice raise in surprised exclamation. "You can't go out there."

Uh-oh! Libby turned sharply and leaned forward to see her friend blocking the doorway with Nick on the other side. Libby slipped farther into the dark corner and froze like a statue.

Nick looked down at the petite brunette blocking his way and impatiently raised an eyebrow. "Excuse me?" He glanced over his shoulder to be sure Roxanne wasn't hot on his trail. She'd been moving closer and closer all night. Damn her. Earlier, he'd decided it was more important to support new businesses than to sulk at home because of the outstanding depositions. New entrepreneurs were always excited, inspiring, and motivating. He resented Roxanne for interfering with his good intentions.

Libby watched and listened, horrified as Dana tried to block Nick with her petite frame. "I wouldn't recommend you go outside. It's much safer inside."

Libby cringed. Improvising was not Dana's forte.

"Safer? Have you seen some of the people in here?" Nick tried to charm the petite guardian and took a step to the side to slide past her. Who was this woman, and why was she standing between him and escape?

"Well, of course." Dana moved to block him. "The mosquitoes, you know. San Francisco just had a reported case of the Zika virus."

Libby wanted to groan. *Zika?* She was ruined.

She watched, frozen, as Nick placed his hands gently on Dana's shoulders and moved her aside. "I'll keep that in mind. Thank you for trying to save my life." He shook his head and stepped outside.

As soon as he was free, Nick rolled his head and neck to loosen the kinks. Damn, but he was tired of this Roxanne business. He glanced again at the door and was relieved she was nowhere in sight. He would wait for Connor's text, telling him the coast was clear. To be safe, he walked to the farthest and darkest corner for solitude, but instead, he ran straight into someone—a female someone.

The woman squealed as he threw her off balance. In the shadows, he could barely make out her silhouette, but he managed to find her bare shoulders, cupping them gently to steady her. As soon as she was still, he released her and took a step back.

"I'm sorry. I didn't see you. Are you alright?" he asked, concerned.

Libby was afraid to talk. *What if he recognizes my voice?* Her bare shoulders tingled where he'd touched them.

"Are you alright?" Nick repeated and squinted. "I can't see a damn thing."

Thank goodness. Libby lowered her voice, "I'm fine," she said, embarrassed by the husky quality of her voice. At least this unexpected attraction disguised her voice "Just had the wind knocked out of me."

"Sorry about that. I thought I was alone out here." Nick tried to peer through the darkness at the woman. From what he could tell, she was medium height, her head reaching him mid-chest, and he knew from catching her that her shoulders were bare. When she didn't respond, he wondered if he was making her nervous. He took another step back. Her silhouette seemed to relax.

"You know," he said, "I have it on the best authority that you're in danger of catching the Zika virus out here."

"So I heard." Libby could not stop herself from laughing. Was that *her* throaty laugh? "Sounds terrifying."

Being taller, a shard of light from inside splayed across a portion of Nick's face. One corner of his mouth kicked up. "That's better."

Confident that he didn't recognize her voice and could not see her, Libby relaxed against the railing where it met the wall. *Stay in the shadows.*

Nick stuck out his hand. "Nick Tremaine."

She hesitated and then reached for his hand in the night. An exciting thrill raced up her arm as his palm engulfed hers. "Um ... Dana Ross," she lied.

He slowly released her hand. He brushed his jacket to either side and slipped his hands into the pockets of his slacks. He rocked back on his heels and peered at the shadowed woman. "Dana Ross."

For some reason, Libby didn't like hearing her friend's name on his lips.

"What brings one Ms. Dana Ross into the terrifying world of the Zika virus?"

"I'm avoiding someone," she said in her lowered voice.

"Ah, then you're in good company. I'm avoiding someone too."

Roxanne, Libby guessed. But feeling brave in her cloak of darkness, Libby laughed and smiled. "Perhaps not the wisest choices for entrepreneurs when we should be networking."

Nick took one step forward, drawn by her voice. "And who are you avoiding?"

She sighed dramatically. "The police. You?"

He played along. "Also the police, I'm afraid. But I'm sure if we wait them out, we'll escape just fine."

"It will be difficult." She warmed to the game. "We don't have any provisions."

He stopped rocking and removed his hands from his pockets. He pointed a finger at her though he wasn't sure she could see his action. "Hold that thought. Don't move." He walked into the ballroom and returned quickly with two glasses of wine. *Roxanne be damned.*

"Some fortitude," he handed her a glass of wine.

"Well done. It was brave of you to risk your cover. Thank you," she said.

He raised the glass and the inner house light glinted

against the glass and the sparkling wine casting a prism along the mystery woman's cheekbone. But just like that, his brief glimpse was gone. "To the police," he cheered.

She tapped her glass against his. "To Zika."

Nick tasted the wine. He was drawn to this woman. "So"—he took a step closer—"who are you really avoiding?"

"A co-worker."

"Male?" he asked.

Most definitely. "Yes. And you?"

"Former employee."

"Female?" she asked for confirmation.

"Yes," he said.

She shivered.

Nick took the wineglass from her hand and turned and placed both of their drinks on the ledge. He shrugged out of his jacket and swirled it around her to settle it on her shoulders. He didn't release his hold on the lapels. "You need this more than me."

She shivered again but for very different reasons. "Thank you," she said as his warmth transferred to her shoulders and arms.

His hands adjusted the collar around her neck. His thumbs brushed smooth skin. A spark surged through him. He paused and finally turned and reached for their glasses. Was he crazy? He was reacting to a woman he had never even seen. But oh, did he want to see her face. "Let's go inside," he invited, his voice lowering an octave with sexual awareness.

"No," she declined gently. Libby tipped her wine and took a deep swallow. She was foolish. What was she doing wearing his jacket and drinking with him? But what else could she do? She couldn't leave and let him see her. She took a deep breath and could almost feel his cologne swirling around her like a spell. He was so close. She knew this was a once-in-a-lifetime experience. She would never have time like this with Nick again. Did she dare sample those lips that had always drawn her attention?

"Are you here as a sponsor or a new entrepreneur?" Nick wanted to know more about her and distract his body and its unexpected reaction to her.

"New entrepreneur," she replied and sipped more wine than was probably wise.

"Congratulations, then. What is your business?" He leaned closer, unable to stop himself.

The heat from his body began to envelop her. Libby hesitated to answer at first and then realized he had Dana's name—what would it hurt to tell this one truth? If anything, she should have made up a name, but it was too late. "Seconds Impressions. It's a speed dating service for business professionals."

He reared back as if to distance himself. "Online dating?"

"No," she said. Knowing Nick as she did, she'd figured he'd have a distaste for internet dating. Besides, as one of the area's most eligible bachelors, he didn't need help meeting women. But maybe he did need help finding the right companion; that was the point of Seconds Impressions. "We interview members who, if approved, sign up for group meetings. They can pick the criteria they are interested in a companion. Their hobbies, for example. We then invite everyone to a restaurant, and each pair has three minutes to talk to each other before they move on to the next person. At the end of the evening, each member selects who interests them. If there is a match, we connect the pair. It's up to them from there."

He studied her shadow for a few silent moments and nodded. "I'll refer a few friends to you that I think would be interested."

"But not you?" she challenged. She was playing with fire. She felt like she was at a masquerade ball or Vauxhall Gardens in South London from one of the many historical romance novels she had devoured.

"Oh, I'm interested, alright, but only in the speed date we are having right here, right now."

"This isn't a date," she teased. "It's a hideout."

"Temporary memory lapse," he chuckled and moved closer still.

"A hazard to your lawless ways," she reprimanded.

He finished off his wine and took her glass. "I'm in trouble anyway."

She didn't pretend to misunderstand. She was definitely in trouble too.

He closed the small distance between them and placed his hands under his jacket on her hips. His thumbs rubbed softly across her hipbones.

She swayed toward him.

He nudged her temple with his nose. He lowered his eyes and found the shadow of her full lips. His voice was thick with desire. "This is crazy. Can I kiss you?"

Drugged with desire, she challenged him by standing on her toes to meet his lips. "I dare you."

He groaned, bent, and dragged his lips across hers. He bit one corner of her lip and then made a slow journey back to the other side. He slid his hands from her hips to her lower back and held her tightly. Damn, but he was aroused already. He swore and settled his lips against hers, taking advantage of her gasp to slide his tongue inside, and then he was done for.

Libby moaned and slid one hand up his chest, over his beating heart and up to cup his head. When he pulled back, she tugged. "Again," she said.

With a tortured groan, Nick brought one hand up to cradle her jaw. With his thumb, he pressed on her chin, opening her lips wide, and then he was there, hot against her. He molded his lips against hers and drove his tongue deep.

She gave a guttural cry into his mouth and thrust her tongue to duel with his.

Some primitive rush roared through Nick, and he wanted to conquer and possess this moment. This woman. Maybe he'd been watching too much *Outlander*.

Libby was mad with lust. She molded herself against him and placed her free hand against his ass to pull him closer. The muscles beneath her fingers flexed with strength. Heaven. Oh, this man.

Nick groaned and tore his lips away from hers. He pushed his leg between hers, or as much as her dress would allow. His jacket slid to the ground. He paved a wet trail down her neck to her bare shoulder and then up to her ear. "Dana, come home with me."

Libby froze and jerked away. Dana's name on his passionate lips amplified what a farce this moment was despite the very real desire coursing through her veins.

Surprised, he lifted his hands. "What—" Before Nick

could figure out what had gone wrong, or if he had scared her (he prayed not), his cell phone started to ring. *Damn.* He knew it would be Connor and that this meant it was an end to the night. He should be relieved it meant he avoided a confrontation with Roxanne, and yet he didn't want to leave this woman standing before him. He grabbed the phone, never taking his eyes off of her shadow.

As she took a step back into the corner railing, he followed. He wasn't ready to let her go. He placed his hand against her hip, closing the distance. He rested his chin on her head. After a second, she curled against him. A good sign, indeed.

"This is Nick," he answered. "Alright. I'll be out front in a few minutes." He put the phone back in his pocket and lifted his head to stare silently at the apparition in his arms.

"Saved by the bell," she teased breathlessly.

He kissed her neck and then her ear. "Come with me."

She shuttered, then shook her head. "I can't."

A loose tendril teased his jaw. *Can't or won't?* He stood straight and with trepidation, trailed his hand down to the ring finger of her left hand. *No ring. What a relief.* He kissed her exposed shoulder. "Come inside, then. I have to leave."

She shook her head again and leaned away from him. "I can't blow my cover." *Literally.*

Frustrated and tired of this mysterious game, he raked his hand through his hair. But he didn't want to push her.

She bent to retrieve his jacket from the ground where it had fallen during their hot-and-heavy make-out session.

He grabbed it first and settled it again on her shoulders. "No, keep it," he said and tugged at the lapels until she was back in his arms. "You're Cinderella but instead of leaving behind a glass slipper, I'll leave my jacket with you. Stay out here as long as you need." He bit her earlobe, and she softened against him. "Leave the jacket with the hostess. I'll pick it up tomorrow, and for both our sakes, leave your number in the pocket. This isn't over." His phone started to ring again. He swore with frustration and kissed her hard on the lips. "I've got to go."

And then he was gone. Libby struggled to regain her composure. He'd called her his Cinderella, and he'd been close to the truth. She thought of her evil stepmother and stepsister. She took off his jacket, hung it over her arm, and let the cool air surround her. She wished he could be her prince.

"Well," Dana said from behind her, "the coast is clear, but from what I think I just saw, you could care less."

Libby turned on her heel and marched toward Dana and tossed Nick's jacket in her arms. "Zika virus? That's the best you could come up with?"

Dana bit her lip. "I was desperate. Well? What did he say when he recognized you? It didn't *look* like he was firing you."

"It was dark; he couldn't recognize me."

"Oh, boy. Then that kiss I might have seen was with whom? Who does he think you are?" Dana finally noticed the jacket in her arms. "What am I supposed to do with this?"

"Give it to the hostess. Nick is going to pick it up tomorrow."

"Why don't you give it to her?"

"Because I borrowed your name."

"You what?" Dana squeaked. "He thinks he was just locking lips with me?!"

"I couldn't very well give him my name, and I didn't have time to think."

Dana huffed. "Looks like I'm not the only one who is bad under pressure." She grabbed Libby's forearm. "Oh, no. The website. Our names."

Libby bit her lip. "I'll call the designer on the way home and tell him to remove my name and bio from the website."

"And pictures. Both of ours," Dana added.

"What a mess." Libby sighed. "I'm sorry."

"Well," Dana teased, "it looked like you were having fun making this mess."

The two friends bumped shoulders as they headed across the ballroom and toward the exit. "Let's get out of here."

"What were you doing while I was on the balcony warding off Zika?" Libby asked. *And turning into a puddle under Nick's lips.*

"I was talking to an attractive gent who I gave my number to. It sounds like I was popular tonight," Dana said with a horrible British accent.

"Ha-ha. Very funny," Libby said. "Who is he?"

"Connor O'Neil," Dana said, smiling.

Libby choked. "Uh-oh."

"Breathe through your nose," Dana said. "If you gulp air in your mouth, it only makes the choking worse."

When Libby gained her equilibrium, she explained. "Dana, he's Nicholas Tremaine's good friend! They were here together."

"Oh, bloody hell," Dana continued with her British farce.

"Bloody hell is right."

Dana wrinkled her nose as if she smelled something bad. "Please don't ask me *not* to see Connor."

Libby sighed. She loved her friend, and since Dana was seldom intrigued by someone, Libby didn't want to interfere. Of course, she wasn't eager to lose her job either. "What if Connor and Nick say they both met Dana tonight?"

The women stared at each other in horror.

"If he calls, I'll come up with some explanation. I'll say you were shy or surprised or not supposed to be there for some lame reason."

"Please don't mention my name to Connor. He'll recognize it from the office. He virtually knows me." She wrapped her arm around her friend. "And he will call you."

Dana nodded. "If you come up, I'll use Beth or Elizabeth. I'll never mention your last name, and I won't share any details about you, of course."

"It's for the best," Libby said, nodding. "I'm looking forward to the day that we can focus full-time on Seconds Impressions and support ourselves with our new venture."

"You and me both," Dana said. "Now, tell me about that kiss."

"What's wrong with you?" Connor asked as Jordan sat silently in the passenger seat. "I worked as fast as I could. Roxanne is a piece of work, man."

Nick looked out the window at the passing lights and snorted. "Yeah, you were too fast this time, my friend."

"Huh?" Connor glanced at his passenger. "Come again?"

"Never mind." Nick was anxious for tomorrow to come when he could pick up his jacket and get Dana's number. "Any luck with the lady you were praising earlier?"

"Definite progress," Connor replied. "What did you think of her? Sexy as hell, isn't she?"

Nick stiffened. "What do you mean?"

Connor spared him a glance. "I saw you talking to her by the balcony."

Nick turned cold. "Who?" Connor couldn't have seen his explosive petting session on the balcony.

"Dana Ross. The lady I'm interested in. I got her number."

"You saw us?" Nick was pissed, but he wasn't sure with whom. Someone was making a fool of him.

"Yeah. What's your problem?"

"When did you get her number?" Nick asked. Something didn't make sense.

"Right before I called you," Connor said. "Why?"

Because Dana Ross couldn't have been in two places at once. "How did you see this Miss Ross and me on the balcony? It was dark."

"No, you were at the door to the balcony."

Ah-ha. The brunette at the door. So whoever he'd been kissing was not Dana Ross. "Damn." He clenched and unclenched his fist. He didn't like being treated like an idiot.

"What's up with you? You're acting put out."

"Sorry, it's the Roxanne thing," Nick lied. Telling his

friend that a woman he liked had given him a fake name wasn't on his to-do list. Connor would rib him forever. "Was your Dana with anyone at the event?"

"She didn't mention if her partner was there, but they started a business called Seconds Impressions."

Yes, his Cinderella had said the same thing: Seconds Impressions. *But why the lies?* She hadn't been wearing a wedding ring. Had she known who he was? Worse, did she know Roxanne Blair? Why would she need to lie about her identity?

Tomorrow wouldn't come soon enough. He couldn't wait to retrieve his jacket and see if she'd left her number. He didn't imagine the chemistry between them. She had felt it too, he was certain. She'd leave her number, he was sure. But if she didn't, he knew where to find her online at least. This was not over.

CHAPTER 10

$\mathcal{T}$he next morning, Libby checked her smartphone one last time. Last night, she'd texted her website designer to make changes to her website ASAP, but he hadn't responded. Her nerves stretched thin as she made her way to the office, even though no one—namely, anyone from Human Resources or Legal—had called her early this morning requesting an emergency meeting, such as one to fire her for making out with her boss last night.

Maybe she was giving herself, or the steamy kiss, too much credit. Perhaps Nick had forgotten about the tryst as soon as he left the event, not curious about "Dana" or seeing her again—unlike Libby, who'd lain awake all night reliving the feel of his lips and body. Maybe he kissed like that all the time. She'd never interacted with him outside of work, so how could she know who he was in his personal life?

All night she'd waffled between fantasizing about his mouth and hands and freaking out that he'd somehow realize it had been her. What if she'd done something to give herself away and the ball just hadn't dropped yet? For all she knew, Nick could be waiting to confront her right now. At the office.

And even if he never discovered that she was his "Cinderella," how could *she* ever look at him the same again? She'd grabbed his ass, for crying out loud. *And what a fine ass.* She'd burned all night, craving his touch, and she had the circles under her eyes to prove it. Libby had never reacted this way, not to any guy. And in just a few seconds, she needed to act like the impersonal, dowdy assistant Nick knew her to be. Being plain and unobtrusive had never felt so unappealing to her.

Libby pressed her cold palms against her warm cheeks and then walked into the office. The lights were on, signaling that he had arrived before her. No surprise there, regardless of the night before. She busied herself with her morning routine of turning on her computer and answering voicemail. *Act like you always do, Libby*, she warned herself as she walked into his office.

He was standing at the floor-to-ceiling window with is back to her, seemingly contemplating the street below.

"Good morning, Mr. Tremaine."

Nick turned shocked eyes in her direction. *That voice. She'd found him.* But no, the phantom surge of recognition and desire faded away when he spotted his dependable assistant. Great, his mind and ears were playing cruel tricks on him. Would he ever find the woman from last night? *Only if she wants me to.* She better have left her number in his jacket pocket.

The change in his expression transfixed Libby. For a

moment, fear clogged her throat. *He recognizes my voice.* But when she saw the intense sparkle fade from his eyes, she tried to relax. He most definitely hadn't discovered Libby and "Dana" were one in these same. Her work disguise was better than she could have ever guessed, but still, she would pause before speaking in the future and moderate her voice.

"Are you alright?" She braved the question, pitching her voice just slightly higher than usual to throw him off the trail. *Be normal. Be normal.*

"Yes, but for a second, I thought you sounded like someone I met last night." His eyes skimmed her pale face and shapeless outfit. "I'm more tired than I thought."

Ouch, Libby thought. He couldn't imagine she'd ever be one and the same.

Nick noticed the shadows under his assistant's eyes. "You look tired too. Are *you* alright?" What did his assistant do in her personal life that created dark circles under her eyes? Reading all night? Watching TV? He knew nothing about her other than she let her hair down at the end of the day. He blinked away the memory of his mystery woman's silky hair and how it had felt to sink his fingers into it.

Libby squared her shoulders and gave him a blank look. "I'm the same as always." *Liar. Liar. Liar.* She wished she could shock him by saying, *"I couldn't sleep all night because I'm still totally turned on, but otherwise, I'm fine."* Her heart was doing the tango, she was sweating like a madwoman under her suit, and her hands itched to grab his ass again. *Argh! Must not grab his ass ever again. Stop thinking about his ass!* "Excuse me, Mr. Tremaine, I have a lot of work to do."

He grunted and took a seat at his desk. "Ms. Duncan?"

She stopped at his door. "Yes?"

"My name is Nick."

"I'm aware of that," she replied and returned to her desk. Now more than ever, she'd be using Nick's surname to enforce distance, for herself if not for him.

Nick flipped on his computer screen. He must have lost his mind last night. He had reacted to a woman like he never had before and was all but obsessing about her—not his usual method of operation. His previous girlfriends would be doing a cheer if they could read his mind right now. Several of them had complained that he didn't seem to think of them as often as he should. Hell, he hadn't slept a wink last night. It didn't sit well with him that the woman had felt the need to lie to him. She'd reacted to his kiss, his touch …Why the lies? He felt obscenely possessive over a woman he knew nothing about. Time to get his jacket and her number. More than anything, he wanted a chance to test his reaction to her, and hers to him. Glancing at his watch, he approached his assistant. "Libby?"

She didn't reply.

"Libby," he said a bit louder.

She still didn't reply.

"Oh for the love of … *Ms. Duncan*," he snapped.

"Yes?" she replied immediately and lifted her face.

Last night had turned him into a bear, and he was looking for a fight. He stalked to her desk and scribbled his suit-jacket brand and color on a sheet of paper. "I attended the New Entrepreneur Gala last night and left my jacket behind. Can you check with the event coordinator and see if someone dropped my jacket off and ask when I can swing by to pick it up?"

Of course, she knew the jacket *had* been dropped off. "You said you weren't going," she accused. *Why was she baiting him like this?*

He scowled. "Should I have called you last night to get permission to change my mind?"

"I'm just surprised to hear you went. I'll find out about your jacket," she said, reaching for the paper as if she weren't concerned, yet anxious for him to move away and take his warmth and hormone-triggering cologne with him. But in her haste to be rid of him, she was clumsy. Instead of grabbing the paper, she clasped his fingers as well. She stifled a gasp, pretending not to feel the spark or remember—with vivid detail—the feel of his skin against hers.

He stared at his hand, then hard at her. Finally, he shook his head as if to clear his thoughts. *Had he felt the spark too,* Libby marveled, a small thrill running through her. Maybe he didn't recognize her, but perhaps he subconsciously did. She should be afraid, but her ego liked the boost.

"I'll have a runner pick up the jacket," she offered and turned back to her computer.

"No!" he all but shouted. "Just find out if it's there. I'll pick it up myself."

Libby read his mind—*he thinks I left my phone number for him.* He *did* want to find her. Heat rushed through her body. Right now, she wished she could have left her number … but she couldn't, and wishing the situation was different was pointless. She hid her reaction to the unintended flattery. Regardless, she soaked it up. Nicholas Tremaine was intrigued by *her*. He just didn't know it.

"I'll let you know what time you can pick it up," she said.

"And adjust my calendar accordingly. Thank you." He went back to his office and closed the door.

Nick rarely closed his door. He was definitely annoyed, she thought, and while part of Libby was pleased to have made an impact on him, her more practical half wondered what he'd do if he ever found out.

Libby scrambled to jump on the internet to check Seconds Impressions' website. *Please, oh, please let the designer have deleted her name.* They'd hired a local college student who typically studied and worked into the wee hours of the morning. It would be just her luck that he hadn't made the changes she'd requested last night.

She hadn't gotten very far when Nick surprisingly threw open his door and walked toward her desk again.

Shoot. She quickly put her screen to sleep. Flushed, she turned toward him. "Can I help you?"

He rounded her desk to stand directly behind her. She schooled her expression and stared blankly up at him. He wasn't looking at her screen, and some of the tension eased from her shoulders. He leaned over her and grabbed another scrap of paper from her desk. Did he have to stand so close? She blanched as he wrote *Seconds Impressions*.

"Can you also find out what in the hell is wrong with this company's website. It says it's 'Under Construction.' Try to find out more about the company and get the partners' contact information, please."

She almost choked. In good news, obviously her designer was updating the site. In bad news, Nick was like a dog with a bone. She'd never mentioned partners to him.

"Partners?" She pulled up her frostiest look and pinched her lips. "Seconds Impressions? I think I've heard of this company. Isn't it a dating service? If this is personal, then" —she slid the note back toward him—"I'd rather not be involved."

Why was she pushing him like this? Her stomach tightened when she realized why. If she was honest, she was peeved at him for not recognizing her. How could two people share the connection they had last night and not recognize each other? Yet, she knew she was ridiculous. And unfair. This was her costume and her subterfuge. And she was risking everything. Ego aside, it was much wiser for her to pretend to research her company rather than risk him finding out any information on his own. At least this way, she could try to manage how much intel he gathered or how quickly he learned anything.

She blushed and folded the note in her hand. "I'm sorry. It doesn't matter if it's personal. I'll look into it."

"No," he said. "You're right. It *is* personal. I shouldn't have asked you. I'll take care of it."

"No, I'll look into it. Actually," she said, "I'm interested in this service as well."

Nick's eyebrows shot to his hairline. "Why Libby, I believe we just had our first personal conversation. We actually have something in common. I just need the partners' info. You don't need to set up a profile for me," he joked.

She pursed her lips and glared at him before turning back to her computer. "That's *Ms. Duncan* to you, *Mr. Tremaine.*" She emphasized the last as much for herself as him.

He chuckled and walked back toward his office. "And that's Nick to you, Libby."

~

Four hours later, Nick stared at the hotel manager as he rechecked the jacket pockets. "You're absolutely sure a note wasn't left when the jacket was dropped off?"

"Mr. Tremaine, if a note was left, I assure you, we would have made sure you received the message."

"And nothing in the pockets?" Nick asked, checking a second time. "Nothing fell out on the floor?"

"We never search pockets, Mr. Tremaine. You have my word."

The event hostess had said the same thing.

Cinderella had ditched him. Frustrated, Nick draped the jacket over his shoulder and walked outside and into the afternoon sun. He grabbed his phone and dialed a board member from the New Entrepreneur committee. "Julie, Nick Tremaine here."

"Nick, it's always a pleasure to hear from you," she said.

"I need a favor. Can you get me a list of attendees from the event last night?"

"We're pretty buried in follow-up tasks for the gala, and not everyone RSVP'd. It might take a few days, but of course."

After thanking her, Nick rang off. Clearly, the passionate woman he'd held in his arms last night didn't want to see him again, and he'd respect her wishes. Nick wasn't about to become a stalker; there were plenty of women eager to date him. But he would find out why she'd given him a fake identity. He wasn't a fool, and he didn't appreciate being treated as one. And he had a sick feeling in his stomach that this all had something to do with Roxanne Blair. He couldn't wait for their lawyers to hash out the truth so he could put Roxanne and the likes of her behind him.

CHAPTER 11

*L*ibby and Dana toured the popular downtown restaurant, deciding how they would situate and decorate the space for their grand opening event to invite people to learn more about Seconds Impressions. After they signed the catering contract, Libby glanced at her watch and cringed.

"Shoot. Dana, I've got to run. I'm late."

"I'll walk with you."

Libby bit her lip as she picked up her pace and went through a mental checklist, patting her pockets. "I feel like I forgot something."

Dana giggled. "You did—the fat check you just wrote and left at the restaurant. Don't worry; it will pay off. The first ad runs today on social media, and the email blast goes out tonight as well."

Libby hoped Dana was right. This event was their first test. Without clients who wanted to participate, it would be a bust. Had they made the right choices for the ad? Would it target their ideal audience?

It was time to put her assistant cap back on. Nick had a meeting starting in ten minutes, and she was supposed to be in it. Only a week into her double career and she was slipping. Now was not the time to change her work habits —her boss had been in a mood ever since he came back with his jacket last week.

He had returned to the office, angry. "Did you find out anything on Seconds Impressions?"

Fortunately, Libby didn't have to lie. "The site is up and running." And without her name or picture anywhere on it. Dana's name and photo remained. They decided Dana's photo was necessary. They needed to include a face for their business, and Nick would figure out Dana wasn't the Dana he met anyway, eventually.

Libby had spied on him from her desk as he returned to his own and tapped on his keyboard. A shiver ran up her spine when she saw his jaw stiffen, and she heard him say, "Will the real Dana please stand up ..."

For both of their sakes, Libby hoped Nick never ran into Dana anywhere. When Libby had updated Dana, she'd only shrugged. "It's out of our hands. We will manage him if it ever happens." And now, a week later, Nick hadn't tried to reach Dana. Not once.

"Dana, I'll call you tonight," Libby said and raced ahead. Her heels clicked against the floor as she entered her building and ran through the foyer.

By the time she reached her office, grabbed her laptop, and headed toward the boardroom, her cheeks were flushed. She wished she could take off her suit jacket to cool down. She waved her hand in front of her face, desperate for air, took a deep breath, and entered the meeting as calmly as possible.

Nick looked up as she entered and then took a quick double-take, frowning.

She grimaced in apology for being late, but he continued to frown at her. She took the seat next to him as usual. She avoided his eyes while she set up her laptop.

"Nick?" the Senior Vice President of Operations prompted.

Nick turned slowly from Libby to the VP. "Sorry, Frank, what was that?"

Libby started taking minutes, all the while aware of Nick's curious regard. She was no longer worried that he might recognize her from the gala, even though it bothered her ego a little bit that he didn't. However, it was more annoying that he kept looking at her now, and he clearly was none too happy with her. Okay, so she was late to *one* meeting. She'd never been late before, and she wouldn't be again. *Get over it, Nick.*

After a while, Nick leaned toward Libby to whisper in her ear so as to not disrupt the meeting.

She held her breath and did her best to ignore the way her skin tingled as his warm breath brushed her ear and neck, teasing its way past her starched collar. Her nipples hardened, and goosebumps ran up her arms. Thank goodness for her jacket. She let her breath out slowly.

"Can you read back the last action item?" Nick asked softly.

She kept her eyes on the screen but leaned her head to the side to whisper back, "Frank will be appealing the city ordinance on height restrictions on October twenty-eighth."

When he remained silent, she glanced at him for further direction. She almost gasped when she found his face immediately before her. Their noses were a hair's breadth apart.

And he was staring intently at her eyes.

Surprised to find him so close, she stared back at his bright eyes rather than glance away. She had never been this close to him—well, not in the office anyway. He had mesmerizing eyes. Her eyes made a quick path over his face and across his lips, recalling how they'd felt. She moved back a few inches and nervously reached to adjust her glasses; only they weren't there. *Oh no! Her glasses!* She *had* forgotten something at the restaurant—part of her costume. No wonder Nick was behaving so strange. She dared another look, and yep, he was still peering at her.

Libby glanced around the room, but no one else was looking at her like she'd grown an extra head. She tried to pay attention for the next hour and take accurate notes. How could she forget her glasses? What could she say to him, and she knew he would ask as soon as he got a chance. And the tricky jerk must have realized immediately, and he'd asked her to read back her notes. He knew she didn't need glasses. *Ugh-ola.*

Nick couldn't focus on the meeting, only his assistant. At first, he'd been amused by his puzzling assistant when she entered without her eyeglasses and her cheeks rosier than usual. His first thought had been, *My assistant of eleven months doesn't need glasses!* He'd seen her take her hair down every night in the bus line, but never her glasses. First the hair. Now the eyewear. Why did she wear the ridiculous things? He'd thought it would be interesting to test her vision by asking her to read some minutes back to him, at least until he'd leaned into her. When she'd turned to him to answer, and with their noses almost touching, Nick had experienced a heady sensation, a familiar one. As if he had been in this position before. Nick inhaled the scent of her breath. No one was more shocked than him when he felt a tightening in his crotch. Thank god for the conference room table. His mystery woman flashed before his eyes, and he was worried he was beginning to lose his mind. Even his mousy assistant was reminding him of "Dana." He had to solve the mystery, if only to get her out of his mind.

And what was it with women lately? Ben Johnston's words from the other day came back to him: *Gentlemen, with all due respect, let's just say everything is not as it appears. Never judge a book by its cover.* He'd forced Ben to pick up a sexual harassment package, yet clearly, Ben knew more about Nick's assistant than Nick did.

When the meeting ended, Libby gathered her equipment and hurried back to her desk. She wished she could jump into a cold pool. She was hot and disoriented after sitting close to Nick. She always sat next to him in meetings, but never after imprinting on him like Jacob in *Twilight.* Libby had needed to cross her legs to stop the tingling. Now, safe behind her desk, she glanced at the large mirror and almost screamed. Her cheeks were still flushed, and without her glasses, she looked like a different person. She looked like the real Libby. She yanked open the second drawer and almost cried with gratitude when she found her backup pair of faux spectacles. She settled them on her nose just in time, because Nick walked through the door.

His jaw clenched when he saw the glasses on her face. "In my office, now."

Her pulse was rioting. She prayed her voice sounded reasonable. "You have a videoconference that starts in a minute."

He leaned over her desk. "Don't push me. Cancel the damn thing and then come to my office."

CHAPTER 12

When Libby entered his office, Nick was waiting, arms crossed against his broad chest. The same chest she'd clutched in the dark a week ago.

"Close the door," he said.

She resisted slamming it to release some tension and walked toward his desk. She was about to take a seat but decided that she didn't want the disadvantage of his height. He was already looming over her as it was.

He stopped three feet from her and put out his hand. "Give me the glasses."

"Why? I need them."

"Cut the crap. Give me the glasses."

She pursed her lips, crossed *her* arms, and raised her chin. "I know what you are thinking, but—"

"Libby," he warned, "you have no idea what I'm thinking."

"Ms. Duncan," she corrected.

"Dammit, Libby. Give me the glasses."

She yanked them off and all but threw them at him.

He caught them easily. He opened the arms and then peered through them as he turned about the room. He walked over to his desk and held them before a document and then his computer screen. His jaw clenched as he gritted his teeth. "These are glass."

"Hence the name *glasses*," she said.

"Clear glass," he accused. "Nonprescription."

She was tempted to say, *What are you now? An optometrist?* But she wasn't stupid and lifted her chin.

"Who are you?" he snapped back. "What in the hell is going on?"

"All of this over a pair of glasses? This is ridiculous," she scolded. Inside, she was shaking. She could not lose this job yet. Seconds Impressions hadn't even held their first event, let alone turned a profit.

"It's not just the glasses. What about the hair when you leave here?" He swung his arm toward the window behind him.

She gasped in horror. "The hair?" she brushed her hands over her head to make sure every piece was in place. She glanced at the window behind him and sucked in a second deep breath. She marched over to it and looked down at the sidewalk where her bus line formed. She turned on her heels and glared at him. "You've been spying on me. You knew all along!"

"No," he roared. "That's just it. I don't know anything. All I know is that my assistant for the past year is in some" —he waved toward her with befuddlement—"costume." He threw a look of disgust at her outfit. "That damn ugly suit is part of it, isn't it?" he barked.

She was so furious she could hardly speak. Nick had watched her countless times from his office window and never said anything. "I have always done a great job for you and so long as I do that, you have no right, absolutely no right, to care how I choose to dress. Other than to expect me to dress professionally, you are in no position to tell me how to clothe myself." She was too angry to feel a pang of conscience over the fact that she had intentionally created this persona for herself. "I'm an excellent employee, and that is all that should matter."

"Women and secrets," he growled.

Libby wasn't about to respond to that.

His jaw clenched, making his cheek spasm. His face looked like it would crack if he so much as moved. He crossed his arms and tucked them beneath his armpits and glared down at her. His voice was cold. "But that's just it, isn't it, *Ms. Duncan*. It's not just the outfit." He took in her angry eyes, inflamed skin, and the stubborn tilt of her chin. *Hell,* he thought, *her voice doesn't even sound the same.* It resembled … He shook his head; there he went again, looking for his mystery woman in everyone else. His assistant's deception didn't help. "You have been playing some damned game and created an identity for yourself here, one that is complete bullshit. I want an explanation. I deserve one."

She flinched and something flashed in her eyes. Guilt? Embarrassment? He didn't know but he couldn't stop. "Ben Johnston knows, doesn't he?"

She blanched. She didn't answer. She had no desire to get Ben or anyone else in trouble.

"He does, doesn't he?!" he roared. "You've made me look

like an idiot in front of my employees. I want answers now."

"I have done a good job for you ..." she started again. Her voice sounded weak even to her ears.

He walked up to his desk and slammed his hand down on it. "Now, dammit. Answers!"

Libby had never seen him like this. His outburst startled her, but she refused to cower.

Nick surprised even himself. He turned from the desk and crossed the room, putting distance between them. He raked a hand through his hair and took a deep breath. And then he stilled, almost frozen. "Does this have anything to do with the Roxanne Blair case?"

Yes. No. Libby paled and dropped into the chair, her anger replaced by shame. She had to tell him the truth, but how much? "Kind of."

"'Kind of'?!"

"Nick, I can explain."

"So now it's 'Nick,' huh?" He marched back to his desk and grabbed the phone, requesting the extension for Human Resources.

Libby leaned across the desk and disconnected the call. "Please. Put the phone down."

Nick looked like he wanted to throw the phone across the room.

"Sit down, and I'll explain." She had recovered her calm voice, yet it seemed to aggravate him further.

His knuckles were white against the handset. "You are in no position to order me about."

"And you"—she raised her voice—"are in no position to be a complete pigheaded jerk."

He set the cradle down with tempered frustration. Sitting down, he leaned back and glared at her. "Start talking."

"I had been looking for a job for two months—" she started, but he interrupted.

"Spare me your life history and jump to the Roxanne Blair part," he growled.

Fine. "I would never have gotten past Melissa Bancroft and Personnel if I had dressed any other way." She stared him in the eye and refused to back down. It was the truth and they both knew it.

Some of the tension eased out of his shoulders as he recognized the truth in her statement. He nodded curtly. "You're probably right. But you've been on board for almost a year now. Why didn't you drop the farce?"

She shook her head with annoyance. "It would have raised too many questions."

"And your personality? And don't give me any crap that you are 'naturally serene,' since you just proved otherwise."

The embers of her temper started to glow again. "It is my work personality. Almost everyone is different at work than they are in their personal lives. Besides, I thought we worked well together."

"Ms. Duncan?" he challenged.

She knew it was a question. "To enforce professional distance. After your experience with Roxanne ..."

He snorted and came out of his seat. He jabbed a finger in her direction. "Don't even make this out to be a favor to me."

"I wouldn't," she replied. "But it's the truth." *Some of it, anyway.* Now was not a good time to tell him that Roxanne had once been her stepsister or about her business venture and eventual resignation.

They were silent for several seconds. The anger was still rolling off both of them and then she heard him mumble something. "What?" she asked.

"Damn deceptive women."

Women. Plural. She knew he was referring to the gala.

She lifted her chin. "I don't want to lose my job."

He stood and walked around the desk and leaned against it, staring down at her. "Is there anything else you have to tell me?"

She paused. She should tell him, but … "Not now." And she meant it—now was not the time to tell him everything. Only, he relaxed, seemingly misunderstanding her statement to say, *Not anymore.*

"Tomorrow," he bit out. "You start dressing as if you aren't hiding something."

He still didn't understand that he had no right to tell her how to dress as long as she did her job. "Have you been happy with my work?" she challenged.

"Yes," he said immediately.

"Then I will dress as I choose." She stood and walked toward the door.

"Libby." His voice sent chills up her spine. "Do not push me on this. Do it in steps, say you had a makeover, do it however you damn well need to do it, but you will drop this damn costume if you want to keep your job. If Ben Johnston knows, what happens if more employees see you outside of the office? They'll speculate you dress the way you do because you're afraid I'll hit on you, and it will fuel the Roxanne Blair rumor mill."

Her jaw dropped, closed, opened again, and then snapped shut. She felt defensive, backed into a corner by her own choices, and she came out fighting—fighting someone she knew could handle what she gave. She stormed to her desk and grabbed her purse. She marched to his doorway. "I'm leaving for the day," she said. She stabbed a finger toward the window behind him. "Enjoy the show."

He put his hands on his hips and peered at her. "I'll *see* you in a few minutes."

Exactly six minutes later, Nick looked down the four flights to see his furious assistant storm onto the bus line. She dropped her bag haphazardly before her and spun on her heels to stare up at him or where he figured she assumed he was standing.

Although he knew she could not see him past the window's reflection, he could feel her defiance. He glared right back at her, and then he stilled.

Libby stared brazenly up at him as she removed the pins from her hair, and it slid over her shoulders. She was already sans glasses. She took her jacket off and let it slip to the ground.

From the four stories above, he could imagine her licking her lips as she proceeded to unbutton her blouse. If Roxanne Blair thought she was sexy with her overt sensuality, she'd never seen someone like Libby Duncan in action.

"Holy ..." Nick swore. She was doing a damn striptease in public. He was furious, and if he weren't so fascinated with what she might do next, he would storm through the building, run outside and throw his jacket over her shoulders.

His heart rate doubled. By the time she had released third button, he was aroused. The damn drably dressed fireball was giving him a raging hard-on. Not expected!

Even after she had spun around and jumped on her bus, Nick was still hard as hell. Damned if he hadn't just gotten a glimpse of the real Libby Duncan. *Women.* They were full of surprises and two had caught him off guard in one week. If Roxanne Blair could see him now, she'd have a field day. He'd never responded to Roxanne. Not remotely. His only interest had been professional.

Roxanne Blair. Damn. He couldn't wait for the depositions to be over. When it came to Roxanne, he was innocent, but he wasn't feeling so professional or innocent right now because he was very much looking forward to seeing Libby tomorrow.

CHAPTER 13

Before he left the office, Nick stopped by Human Resources. They kept the wing locked after hours, and the team was gone, but he had a master key. At home, Nick reviewed Libby's personnel file. Everything Libby said checked out. Her background security check was solid. Her references were glowing, and her past employment had been verified. Naturally, nothing mentioned her appearance outright other than to say she was highly professional. The biggest surprise had been that Libby was short for Elizabeth; even her reference letters referred to her as Libby. At least she'd opted to use her common name at the office even if he'd been the only one not allowed to use it. He dialed his personnel director's cell number.

"Sorry to bother you at home, Melissa, but I have a question about Libby Duncan."

"I hope everything is alright."

"When you interviewed her, what was your first impression?"

Melissa didn't answer right away, and then she sighed. "Off the record?"

"Maybe."

"I had already reviewed her resume and letters of reference, but once I *saw* her, I was positive she would be the perfect fit."

"That's what I needed to know."

Libby had been right. She'd anticipated a need to look like someone who'd never hit on her boss. Right or wrong, it's what had happened.

"What's going on?" Melissa asked. "Was I wrong? Please tell me I wasn't wrong."

"No, you were spot on. She is perfect." Nick learned years ago not to keep information from his senior team, especially HR. "She's been playing her looks down, wearing glasses she doesn't need."

Melissa said, "So she either has been harassed before, or she'd heard about Roxanne Blair."

Nick realized then that by rushing Libby to explain her get-up, she hadn't told him how she knew HR would be looking for a non-threatening, yet highly qualified, executive assistant. He would ask her tomorrow. If they were going to work together, they needed to be honest. That was, if she wasn't too pissed to return to work.

Melissa continued, "It's not a huge surprise if it's the latter. Recruiters talk, and we know Roxanne has been talking for months."

"Unfortunately," Nick said.

"Is there anything I need to do? Do you want me to talk to her?" Melissa asked.

"I've encouraged her to make some adjustments so she'll be more comfortable at work—the facade isn't necessary. She's proved her professionalism and ability to separate work from her personal life." *Or they both had up until a few hours ago.* He thought about her exaggerated unveiling when she waited for the bus. He owed her an apology.

"I'll pull her aside tomorrow. I'm sorry, Nick, that I, my team, including any recruiters we sourced, gave her the impression that it was necessary to play a part. She was the most qualified candidate, and I'd like to say that I would have hired her no matter how she looked. But her appearance was a relief."

"Thanks, Melissa. I appreciate your candor. Talk to her tomorrow, and let's all move forward and avoid concerns like this in the future." There was a knock at his door. "I've got to run. See you tomorrow at work."

When he opened the door, he wasn't surprised to see his friend Connor, who regularly showed up with little notice or often unannounced, but he was surprised by Connor's goofy grin as opposed to his typical taciturn expression. "Someone's happy," Nick said, stepping aside invitingly.

Connor smiled all the way to the bar, making himself comfortable and pouring a dash of brandy. "I'm crushing. Hard."

"Who are you, and what have you done to Connor?" Nick joked. "Crushing?"

"I feel like a kid again. Remember Becky Been?"

Whoa. Becky Been had been Connor's first crush in the third grade. Though Connor had grown up in London, their parents had been close, and Nick had known him his entire life. He had the pen pal letters to prove it. "Don't tell me you found Becky Been?" Nick asked, grabbing a drink of his own.

Connor loosened his tie and slid lower into the couch. "Of course not. Better."

Better? "This is getting interesting," Nick said.

"Dana, the woman from the gala," Connor said. "I just saw her again. She makes me laugh. Who knew a great sense of humor could be such a turn-on?" Connor asked, genuinely perplexed.

Nick shook his head. First, he didn't want to go down a pity-party rabbit hole being annoyed about his unfound mystery woman, who had stolen Connor's siren's name and refused him her number. Second, he doubted his friend had ever tried to have a real conversation with a woman. Connor never had to talk. For as long as Nick could remember—and it was a long time—Connor could step into room and women threw themselves at him with little to no interest in talking. And if he did say anything, his British accent made them swoon.

Nick only hesitated briefly before asking, "Does Dana have any friends?"

"Loads, from the sounds of it." Again, Connor sounded surprised, but of course, Connor could count his friends on one hand.

"I meant single," Nick said dryly.

"Didn't ask. Should I have?" Connor asked.

Nick stared at his friend. Connor had a high IQ, but when it came to the emotional quotient, he often missed subtleties. And humor—which made it all the more impressive that Dana's humor appealed to his friend. Nick would have to be more direct.

"I mean a single friend that I might want to meet. For instance, her partner. Did you ever learn her name?"

"Beth," Connor nodded. "She talks about her a lot."

Beth. The name suited his gala apparition and the breathy quality of her voice. Unfortunately, Beth had made it clear she didn't want to hear from him again despite their chemical combustion. "It's funny," Nick said. "Seconds Impressions' website was down the other day, but when I looked again today, it only listed Dana's name as one of the owners."

"Why is that funny?" Connor asked.

Nick chuckled. "Not funny as in a laugh. Funny as in strange." Yeah, Nick was more curious than ever about Dana's sense of humor and how it managed to get through to his friend.

Connor nodded. "I see what you mean. Why is Beth a silent partner if she was at the gala networking?"

Yes, and why doesn't Beth want me to call her? "Remember when I was on the balcony while you were clearing the way for my escape?" Nick asked Connor.

"Of course," Connor said.

"I met Dana's partner on the balcony, but I didn't get her name." No point in telling Connor that Beth had stolen Dana's name.

"I'll have to ask for Beth's full name," Connor said. "And I'll ask if she is single too. For my friend," Connor said and winked.

"Thanks, Connor. But I asked for her number, and she didn't give it to me."

"Maybe she didn't think you were funny ..." Connor looked at Nick expectantly. Nick roared with laughter.

"Yeah, Connor. Now *that* was funny."

CHAPTER 14

*L*ibby stood before her office door, counting to ten before marching inside to apologize to Nick. She wasn't one hundred percent positive he'd witnessed her rebellion from his perch above, but she felt childish for her actions regardless. She was compromising by ditching her glasses, and while she still wore a bun, it wasn't as tight. If necessary, she might even call him Nick.

Nine, ten. She pushed open the door and stopped dead in her tracks when Melissa stood up from one of the waiting chairs. *I'm fired.*

"Libby." Melissa smiled. "Nick's not here yet. Can we talk for a minute?"

Libby blushed as Melissa's eyes danced over her glasses-less face and more casual hairstyle. *She knows.* Nick had said something.

Melissa led her to the nearby conference room and shut the door, and Libby waited for Melissa to begin. She wasn't about to start her own termination meeting.

"Libby, I'm sorry for the position that I, my team, or our recruiters put you in."

Eyes widening with confusion, Libby asked, "Excuse me?"

"May I be candid?"

"Please," Libby said.

"I talked to Nick last night. He told me you downplayed your appearance so you'd be taken seriously for the role." Melissa leaned forward earnestly. "You were our strongest candidate. You would have gotten the job, but I'm embarrassed to admit that your appearance did make it even easier to hire you. But ultimately, it was your experience and the glowing references you received that sealed the deal. Not your appearance. We put you in an unfair position. And I've made that clear to Nick."

"So, I'm not fired?" Libby asked on an exhale.

"No. No, of course not. If anyone should be worried about her position, it's me," Melissa said.

"Please don't, Melissa. I chose to dress the way I did after hearing about Roxanne Blair's claims from someone outside of the organization. It wasn't you or anyone on your team that gave me the idea to dress as I've been." Libby hoped the woman wouldn't ask further questions. Overnight, she'd come to the conclusion she owed Nick the truth, but she had to find the right time.

But no such luck.

"And this person outside the organization, they didn't try to talk you out of it, or scare you away from the job. Why?"

She'd be honest. "They didn't know I'd apply."

"And Roxanne Blair, does she know you applied?"

"Absolutely not."

"Are you friends with Roxanne Blair?"

"Absolutely not," she said and then paused to choose her next words carefully. "I knew her once, but I haven't seen or spoken to her in decades."

"And how did you know her?" Melissa asked.

This was the moment. This would be the information that would get Libby canned.

But just then Nick glided past the glass-enclosed conference room, his step slowing as he recognized the pair. With his expression giving nothing away, he poked his head inside and asked, "All settled here?"

Melissa stood up. "We're great. Right, Libby?"

Libby met Melissa's stare, the unanswered question from before left hanging, and turned to Nick. "Yes, we are great."

"Good, let's get to work." And with that, Nick turned and walked toward his office.

Melissa held the door open for Libby. "Thank you, Libby, for trusting me."

Libby smiled with relief. "And thank you for trusting me."

By the time Nick reached his office, his pulse had slowed a bit. Though he'd known Melissa wanted to apologize to Libby, he hadn't expected her to approach his assistant first thing in the morning. Walking in and seeing the two in the conference room, well, Nick had been certain that Libby was handing in her resignation. He wouldn't have accepted it. He'd hoped to meet Libby early as usual, apologize for his anger yesterday, tell her she could dress however she chose, and pretend he'd never seen her sidewalk striptease the night before. Everyone knew how difficult it was to find an excellent executive assistant. And he was no fool.

And no matter how much it pleased him, he wouldn't acknowledge that she wasn't wearing the glasses or tight bun. He assumed her efforts were an olive branch, and he was greedily going to take it.

Melissa and Libby had said everything was fine. He could stop worrying about his assistant's curious choices and focus instead on his real mystery woman, Beth.

CHAPTER 15

I want to be there when you question Nick and the team, so that I can correct them," Roxanne said to Luke.

"That's not the way it works," Luke said while adding his files to his briefcase. "Do you trust me?" he asked, his eyes sweeping over her red jumpsuit. "Do you only own red clothing?"

If she admitted it to herself—and she did—she was glad he had noticed what she wore. Nick had never commented on her clothing before.

Luke repeated himself. "Do you trust me?"

Roxanne hesitated—not because she didn't trust him, but because, oddly, she realized she did. Over the past few weeks, she'd thrown every fit and challenge his way, but he'd remained calm and collected and had moved the case forward. He'd never once looked at her like the other attorneys had. Like she had deserved to get fired. Nor had he implied that she had been some money-hungry bitch. "I do."

"In that case, I've got this. It may not turn out the way you *think* you want it to, but—"

"What?"

"But," he said, "I will get to the truth of the matter. This is a process, Roxanne, and one I intend to handle with the same care I use for all of my clients' cases."

"Luke, what do *you* believe, though? What does your gut say?"

"I don't work by my gut," he said. Luke took in her hopeful expression. She was looking for validation that he couldn't give her until he'd met with Nicholas Tremaine. And yet he found himself saying, "My hunch says Nicholas Tremaine treated you in a way that most men haven't." *With professional courtesy and respect.* Luke had been reading up on Tremaine for weeks now, and he didn't strike Luke as a man who needed authority to get a woman. Not any woman. His hunches said that Roxanne's self-worth was low, and it wouldn't take a lot to misinterpret Tremaine's intentions. But he kept these thoughts to himself. By the end of today, he'd know if his instincts were right.

She crossed her arms and pouted. "But I will go mad waiting around all day. Mad."

He closed his briefcase and swung the leather strap over his shoulder. "Go and do something that will take your mind off of things. Call a friend to wait it out with you."

"I don't have money for shopping, and I don't have ... I don't have any friends."

Luke paused. None? How did a woman like Roxanne end up so alone in the world?

"What about your dad?" The same dad who had called in a favor for Luke to help her.

She shook her head. "He's golfing or something."

Luke pulled out his phone and dialed a friend. When she answered he asked, "Full house today? Can you use some help?" After he hung up, he wrote down a name, address, and phone number and handed it to Roxanne.

"Aging Out & Onward?" Roxanne read aloud. "What's this?"

"It's a nonprofit organization that helps foster kids who turn eighteen and are no longer wards of the states, and therefore, are turned out to the streets."

Roxanne couldn't believe her ears or the twinge she felt in her heart. It had been a long time since she'd felt empathetic. "At eighteen? Are you kidding me? Doesn't the government help them go to college? Or what about finding a job and shelter?"

Luke seemed to be pleased with her questions because he nodded his head and smiled at her. "Head over there now. They'll explain their mission. They can use your help."

When he reached his office door, she asked him softly, "Luke? Do you really think I have something to offer them?"

He turned and stared hard at her. "I *know* you do."

CHAPTER 16

*D*ays passed, and Libby couldn't believe she still had her job. Nick had been extremely professional with her, never once mentioning her relaxed appearance or her performance the other night. And if Melissa had updated him on the details of their discussion and that Libby once knew Roxanne, he didn't seem to care. She had already decided that if he asked her any questions about Roxanne, she'd tell him everything. But as it turned out, Melissa seemed content with *when*, and not *how*, Libby had known Roxanne. She felt a bit guilty, still, not telling them she'd once been related to Roxanne and that she remained close to Roxanne's aunt, Grace. But maybe no one wanted to rock the boat, including Libby, so she let it go. Besides, they had the depositions with Lukas Cooper beginning today. They needed to show solidarity. Fortunately for Libby, she didn't have to worry that Roxanne would be in attendance and recognize her. Her attorney was coming alone.

And Libby was on her way to get Lukas Cooper from

the lobby now. She was curious about what she'd think of him. And despite knowing they would come out ahead, she was still nervous. Roxanne had always seemed to get whatever she wanted, and Libby hoped she wouldn't get it at Nick's expense. Lukas Cooper had a stellar reputation as a man who always wins his fight.

A broad-shouldered man with a square jaw stood in the lobby. "Mr. Cooper?" Libby asked.

He smiled and extended his hand. "Yes. Melissa Bancroft?"

Libby shook her head. "No. I'm Libby Duncan, Mr. Tremaine's assistant. If you follow me, I'll take you to the conference room where you can perform the depositions. Our legal representative will be in attendance."

Luke nodded and followed Tremaine's assistant. She was pretty. A softer and more subdued beauty than her predecessor. And not a dot of red in her clothing.

Once he was settled, and she'd returned with a coffee for him, he asked, "Do you like working for Nick Tremaine?"

Legal hadn't arrived yet, and Libby knew she wasn't on the deposition list. Since she had nothing to share but a positive opinion, she said, "He's the hardest-working man I've ever worked for."

"How long have you worked here?"

"A year this week," she said.

"You're aware of Roxanne Blair's claims?"

"Yes," she said.

"Believe her?"

Libby met his stare. She knew she only had one chance to get this right without giving away too much. "Nicholas

Tremaine is a man of integrity, and no one, I mean no one, respects their employees more than Nicholas Tremaine respects his."

Luke looked past her. "Here comes the man of the hour now. Thank you, Libby."

"It's Ms. Duncan, Mr. Cooper."

"Thank you, Ms. Duncan," Lukas Cooper corrected.

"Good morning, Ms. Duncan. Mr. Cooper, I presume?" Nick said as he entered.

Libby stepped out so the men could introduce themselves and get busy. Oddly, Nick looked like he was blushing, but why? He caught her staring at him. She nodded and left.

Nick was glad to meet Lukas Cooper in person. Under different circumstances, he might actually like the guy. He respected him on paper, at any rate. His name was associated with several local charities, particularly those that helped the indigent. Successful in his own right, he must be good at his job. Nick was relying on Cooper's common sense to see through Roxanne and dismiss her claims once and for all.

After Cooper explained he would be interviewing several employees, including Nick, to corroborate information, they addressed the timing of Roxanne's employment, and Lukas got straight to the point.

"While in your employment, were you attracted to Roxanne Blair?"

"No."

"Did you ever think of Roxanne Blair in a sexual manner?"

"No." Nick was glad that the question was specific because if Cooper had asked him if he ever thought about his *assistants* sexually, he'd be in trouble. Last night, he'd dreamt of one Libby Duncan, lying in his bed, her blond hair hanging and teasing his bare stomach ... Now was not the time to be replaying that dream. No time was the right time.

"Did you ever touch Roxanne Blair?"

"Except to shake her hand sometimes, no."

"Did you try to kiss Roxanne Blair?"

"Never."

"What did Roxanne Blair wear to work?"

Nick was sure that Cooper was trying to trick him, but he had nothing to hide. "Something red. Red is all she wore." Everyone knew that.

And the questions continued.

Nick was relieved when they finished an hour later. Even knowing his innocence when it came to Roxanne, he was exhausted. He felt horrible that some of his employees would have to go through this on his behalf.

When he walked into his office, he appreciated that Libby knew him well enough not to pepper him with questions. She left him alone in his office until his calendar dictated otherwise. Little did she know, though, that she'd given him the patience he needed when he first entered the deposition because he had heard her praise about him to Lukas Cooper, and he would value her high regard always. Libby Duncan may have her silly disguise, but she would never lie about her opinion of him. And she'd made Lukas

Cooper call her Ms. Duncan. Nick leaned back in his chair and smiled.

~

Hours later, Libby poked her head into Nick's office. "I just walked Lukas Cooper out."

He sat back in his chair and sighed. "Good. How's the team?"

She shrugged. "I haven't had the chance to check on them. I wanted you to know first."

"What was Cooper's mood like when you walked him out?"

"Same as when he arrived."

"Suppose that's part of being a good lawyer. Wouldn't want to play a game of poker against him."

Libby simply nodded. "I suppose not."

"God, I hope this over soon."

"It will be." Libby couldn't explain why, but she'd liked Lukas Cooper, and she wanted to believe he could see through her ex-stepsister. And maybe, just maybe, he'd help Roxanne in some way. She didn't know why she had a good feeling about him or his intentions, but she did. He seemed fair. But as Nick had implied, he probably had a great game face as a lawyer.

Nick glanced at his watch. *Almost five.* "I want to recognize the team's efforts. This isn't a cause for celebration, but I do want to thank them for taking time away from their work for this. And it's been a long day." He picked up the phone and made a three-way call on speaker. "Melissa, Jim, how about dinner? Round up any of your team that is able to come at short notice. This isn't a celebration, mind you, but a thanks for their hard work."

"Sounds wonderful," Melissa said.

"Good idea," Jim said.

Libby was just turning to rush to her desk and scramble to find a place for the team to meet when Nick stopped her.

"I got this. You're invited too. None of us could have gotten through today without you. Ordering lunch for everyone was smart. And the bottle of Advil next to the catering? Brilliant." Within seconds, he had a private room reserved at Restaurant Aurora.

Must be nice to have connections, she thought. The restaurant gave Libby pause. It was the perfect choice for a work dinner, but hard to get into without a reservation. In fact, it was a venue where she was hoping to host a Seconds Impressions event in the future, but she hadn't had a chance to see the new restaurant herself. As much as she hated to break her rule against attending after-hours work events, she couldn't resist this opportunity. Dana would be thrilled about the preliminary surveillance.

"So, what do you say, Ms. Duncan? Will you have dinner with us?"

Libby hesitated only a second before smiling. "Yes, I will."

CHAPTER 17

*R*oxanne paced the waiting area at Luke's office. She couldn't wait to talk to him. Couldn't wait!

James, Luke's assistant, tried one more time, "I don't know if he's coming back to the office today."

"But, he did the depositions today."

"That doesn't mean he'll come back here once he's finished. It's past five now."

"I'll wait." Roxanne ignored his raised brows.

"Maybe *I* won't wait," James said, making it clear that in that case, she wouldn't be waiting either. "What then?"

Roxanne nibbled her lip. James needed to cut her some slack. Yes, she wanted to hear about the day, but she also wanted to tell him about her spectacular day at Aging Out & Onward. She'd come straight from the organization to his office. As soon as she'd stepped inside the transition house for young women, she'd felt an odd sort of kinship and understanding for believing there was no one on your side. She'd spent her entire day there, and the time had flown. Almost immediately she spotted a need, a role she could fill, and she couldn't wait to tell Luke about it. She'd spoken to Loretta, the woman in charge, and she'd loved Roxanne's idea to do confidence workshops, sessions where Roxanne could teach the young women to walk tall, dress for success, and she could even teach them simple things, like etiquette. She thought of the scene in *Pretty Woman* when the hotel manager showed Julia Roberts what forks to use and when—Roxanne could teach them so much more!

"James, please. Just a few more minutes. Can you call his cell and ask him when he'll return?" She must have sounded as earnest as she felt because he sighed dramatically and picked up his phone and dialed.

Within seconds, Roxanne heard a ringing coming down the hall, and then Luke walked in. "I'm right here … oh, I didn't expect to see you, Roxanne." Except he sounded like he didn't mean this at all, and he *had* expected her to be waiting. *Men.* Of course she was waiting! Today was the most important day of her life.

"James, feel free to head out and lock up behind you. Roxanne, why don't you come to my office?" Luke wished he could wait for tomorrow to have this talk. Roxanne's face was lit up like a disco ball, expecting life-changing words from him. Well, she'd be getting some, just not the ones she wanted. She could be a major pain in the ass, but he'd grown to like her relentless spunk, and he didn't want to be the bad news bear or her tough-love coach.

"So?" she asked, dropping into the seat before his desk. "Did you make Nick grovel?"

Luke grunted as he pulled files out of his case and slid them onto his desk.

"Or Melissa Bancroft? I would have loved to see you tear her apart."

"I don't tear people apart. I dissect what they say to distinguish the truth from lies and even legitimate lost-in-translation miscommunications."

Roxanne made a blah-blah-blah puppet of her hand. "Hurry up. Tell me the good news because I have other good news to share. They'll settle, right? Or we will go to court?" She leaned forward in her chair, eager.

Luke stared at her gorgeous face and her absolute inability to read his expression or body language. Admittedly, as a lawyer, he was good at hiding his thoughts, but he wasn't bothering to try now. It was a test, and she had failed. He might as well tell her now and get this over with.

"It's over, Roxanne."

She pumped her fist in a very un-Roxanne-like way. "I knew it."

He grunted again. "It's over, as in there is nothing for them to settle, and we don't have a case."

She blinked. "I don't understand. You're the best lawyer in town. My father said so."

He sighed and leaned forward. "Roxanne, it's over. Trust me."

"Trust you?" She jumped up. "But, he harassed me. He did!"

After meeting with Nick Tremaine and his team, and corroborating every statement they had ever given against that of Roxanne's—of which, hers had been inconsistent with other lawyers and HR—he knew that Roxanne had misunderstood respect and professional courtesy as interest. What kind of men were in her past, that someone treating her with kindness and respect could be so misconstrued? If Roxanne's dad was there, Luke might throttle him for his possible contribution to his daughter's self-worth.

"I can't believe you don't believe me," she said, grabbing her purse. Her excitement about AO&O was lost in the weeds of this devastating news. What would she do? She was broke. "I can't even get a job because of what he's done to me. I can't pay my rent, bills …" She looked around the room aimlessly.

Something primal raised in Luke—something he'd ever felt before—and he wanted to sweep her into his arms and rescue her. But she didn't need him to save her; she needed to save herself first.

"Can you stay with your dad for a while?" As soon as she left, Luke would call her father and make damn sure he'd help her. He owed Luke now.

"His new wife hates me."

"Do you have any family you can turn to?" He was starting to get a clearer image of Roxanne facing the world alone. No wonder she never quit.

"Aunt Grace. But I'd be in the way. She always preferred Libby over me."

Libby? Luke's blood chilled. "Who is Libby?"

"My sister. Or she was my sister. Ms. Goody-Two-Shoes' dad married my mom. Didn't last. I even had to go by Roxanne Duncan for a while. My mom changed my name as many times as she changed husbands."

Luke called on the poker face of all poker faces. *Libby Duncan.* Nick's assistant. How did this all fit together? And had he failed Roxanne today? No, he stood by his findings. Libby Duncan had started after Roxanne left. He'd confirmed so with HR. Did Nick know Libby was related to Roxanne? No way. What was going on? As soon as possible, he'd be calling Libby Duncan.

"When's the last time you saw your stepsister?" he asked.

"Decades ago, thankfully." Roxanne would hate for perfect Libby to see what had become of her. Libby was probably an ideal something or other with a dream life in a super place with a perfect family. Her stomach began to turn. "I'm not feeling so well."

Luke jumped to his feet.

Roxanne was growing paler by the second. She slumped in her chair. "I think I'm going to faint," she said breathlessly.

"I'll be right back," Lukas said, rushing for a bottle of cold water from the vending machine down the hall. "Don't move."

What was she going to do now? Tears pooled in her eyes, blurring the file on Luke's desk labeled *Roxanne Blair.* Looking over her shoulder to make sure he wasn't returning, Roxanne reached for the file and flipped through it. All the names were familiar, but the last one was unexpected: *Libby Duncan, Executive Assistant to N.T.*

She almost dropped the file. "Oh god." The room rolled before her. Libby? Libby had her job? And Luke had just pretended he didn't know anything about her! They'd conspired against her. All of them. She'd been played the fool, treated like a pretty idiot. How the two had come together, she had no idea, but he had lied to her and betrayed her with her perfect ex-stepsister—just when she was starting to trust someone. Hands shaking, she put the folder back on his desk and stood. A wave of dizziness hit her just as Luke returned.

Luke lunged forward to grab Roxanne's arm to help steady her. *Shit.* Right now, Luke was going to follow his rescuer instinct after all, but with some tough love because, dammit, he wanted this woman to be able to rely on herself and keep her spunk.

"Enough of a pity party," he said and put up his hand when she was about to melt down before his eyes. "Listen, I will give you a job. James is going on month-long vacation. You can work here in his absence. If you're any good, you can stay on. Call me crazy, but if you want an opportunity to rebuild your resume, you can start here."

"Me? Work for you? If I'm such a horrible person, why would you let me work for you? Don't you think I'll 'lie' about you too?" She glared at him with such hatred, he almost stepped back.

"I never said you lied." Placing his hands on her shoulders, he turned her so he could meet her eye for eye. "I think you've been treated like shit by too many men to count, and when Nicholas Tremaine treated you as a human being, you thought it meant more."

Roxanne's heart dropped to her stomach, and her face grew slack. She hated pity. Tears pooled in her eyes. She'd never thought about her life like this, but something about it hurt. Something like a gut-level truth she hadn't realized existed. And worst of all, it was coming from a liar. "No."

"Yes," Luke said, and to his surprise, he tried to pull her into a hug except like a furious cat, she lashed out with her claws and then slapped him. "You're the worst of them all. I trusted you!" she cried and ran out of his office.

CHAPTER 18

*L*ibby looked around the table at the full, relieved, and relaxed group. Nick had set the tone upon arrival, thanking the team for all they had done for him and Tremaine Development.

"No matter what happens next," Nick said, "you'll always have my deepest respect for your work ethic and my appreciation for your trust in me. Thank you."

There'd been no champagne or cheers; everyone knew that for every winner, someone must lose. But well-earned bottles of chianti had made their way around the table.

Libby had been mesmerized by Nick all night, having never seen him outside the office, well, except for the New Entrepreneur Gala. *But enough of those thoughts.*

He was so charming, effortlessly engaging the group in non-work discussions. Libby was touched and impressed; he appeared to know the names of all the spouses and children. At one point, he asked Jim, "What are you getting Molly for your thirtieth anniversary?" And when Jim winked and said the best present he could get for his wife was an advanced copy of Natalie Kimby's latest novel, Nick had said, "I'm positive my aunt would love to help."

First, Libby was surprised his aunt was an author, even if Libby had never heard the name before. Second, she was touched when Nick excused himself to text his aunt and make the arrangements.

"She loves the idea. She'll have a copy for you in a month."

Jim shook Nick's hand across the table. "You're my hero."

Libby couldn't help but wish he could be her hero too. *Gorgeous. A great kisser. And kind ...* She shook her head. *Stop that. He's your boss.*

The group was growing quieter now. Libby knew it would only be a matter of minutes before the first person made their excuses and left. She looked around for the restaurant manager. As soon as everyone left, she'd introduce herself and talk about future business.

Melissa was first. "Time to go. I have a teen who probably hasn't started her homework."

"I'll walk you out," Jim said.

"Anyone need a cab? On me," Nick said.

Nick had long since taken care of the bill. He signaled the hostess for his jacket. The rest of the group stood, shook hands, and started to say their goodbyes, Libby included. As soon as everyone turned to go, Libby excused herself, saying she needed to use the restroom. "I'll see you all tomorrow."

She took her time in the restroom. If she'd known this could happen tonight, she would have brought some blush and lipstick, anything to make her look more like a partner in a business, rather than a pale, tired assistant, but alas, she'd make the best of it. It would be weird to let her hair down since the manager had seen her already, but she took off her jacket and loosened her collar. Glancing at her watch, she was reasonably confident that taxis and valet would have seen everyone off. It was time to make a second impression. *Pun intended*, she thought and smiled.

Nick returned to the restaurant to wait for Libby. It was late, and he knew she would need a ride home, after all, she had taken the bus to work and carpooled to the restaurant.

He'd enjoyed the night. He respected the hell out of his team, and not because they supported him. They were nice people. Good people. Tonight had also been the first time he'd seen Libby outside of work. Sitting across the table from her, he caught her watching him a few times, and he had wished he could ask what she was thinking. And there was no reason he couldn't have, except his gut said she wouldn't like having the group's attention drawn to her. More of a listener, maybe even a people-watcher, she hadn't said much, but when she did, the team listened. At one point, she'd exchanged a few puns with Jim, and the two laughed together quietly. His assistant had clearly established relationships, one-on-one, with his team. He was impressed.

The bar was near the door, and he took a seat on a high stool to wait for her. Shaking the bartender off, he wished he could actually be having a nice glass of wine, and his thoughts drifted to the apparition he'd held and kissed at the gala. So far, Connor hadn't been able to get Beth's last name out of Dana, which made it all more suspicious. What was Beth hiding? Okay, so she'd made it clear she didn't want to hear from him, but his gut said something was off. He did not imagine the chemistry. The restaurant was growing empty, and just then, he heard Libby's voice floating down the hall. He followed the tone and recognized her silhouette as she spoke to the manager. They were having an avid discussion if he was reading their body language right. Libby stuck out her hand, and the manager shook it firmly.

"I'll see you next week," Libby said, smiling wide as she turned toward the door.

Whoa! Nick felt sucker punched. Libby's smile was brilliant. It changed her entire face. Not to mention her blouse was unbuttoned, similar to the way she had challenged him that day from her bus line. He moved uncomfortably in his seat. *Calm down, Nick.*

Libby froze when she saw him. "What ... what are you still doing here?"

"I wanted to make sure you got home okay." Nick's voice was rough when he spoke. *Dammit.*

Libby opened her mouth and then closed it. Speechless, it seemed.

He stood, letting his jacket hang before his crotch. *When had he become such an adolescent?*

"That's so kind," Libby began. "But I can get an Uber or Lyft."

Nick reached for her elbow. "It's no problem. Valet is keeping my car warm," he said, nodding toward his Tesla at the curb.

For lack of anything else to say, Libby said, "I didn't know you had a Tesla." Another point in his favor. Earth-friendly. *He's becoming my dream man*, she thought. She wondered if he'd noticed her blouse and if she should slyly rebutton it. Self-conscious, she slid into her jacket as he led the way through the door.

Once they were settled, and he started driving, the music kicked in. *The Civil Wars. Darn, another point in his favor.* Maybe one glass of chianti was enough around the man because Libby worried if she kept up this tally, she might just fall for him. Hard.

"What were you talking to the manager about?" Nick asked her.

He didn't sound suspicious, but honestly curious, and Libby wished she could tell him the entire truth. She was tired of lying. Tired of acting less exciting and interesting than she really could be. Her dad, and probably a million other people, used to say, "There's no time like the present." She couldn't bear to add another lie to her list, so she said, "I ... I have a side business I'm trying to build."

Nick's eyes widened, but he didn't take them off the road. He turned the radio off. "Fascinating. You're a secretive one," he said.

If you only knew.

"Thank you for telling me. I won't press you for more, but if you'd like to tell me more about it, I've been told I'm pretty damn good at advising new entrepreneurs."

She wondered if he was thinking about the New Entrepreneur Gala.

And it was because of the gala that she couldn't tell him. To tell him now that her business was Seconds Impressions

... utter sabotage. Roxanne Blair's claim was still on the table. No one knew what Lukas Cooper's next steps would be. Confiding in him now would put them both in a horrible position, one of her making. So instead, she said, "I will tell you more about it someday, but not yet. It's just taking off."

"Libby," he said, sounding genuine to her ears, "at the risk of sounding condescending, I'm proud of you."

She turned and looked at his profile. *Another point. Cripes.* She was falling. Fast.

"And I won't hold it against you." He paused and cleared his throat. "That is, I expect you will be successful and that will mean your resignation is a matter of *when* not *if.*"

Libby felt tears rush to her eyes. He was killing her with kindness. What would he do if, no when, she eventually told him the truth?

Nick was glad they were quiet for the rest of the trip. Too much was going through his mind. He was proud of her, but not himself. He was drawn to his assistant for some inexplicable reason. She was like a cat. The more she warmed up to him, the more honored he felt, and the more he wanted.

"I'm here," Libby said, pointing to her building.

Nick double-parked but didn't move to get out of the car. He didn't dare. Blame the chianti, or blame the sexy woman next to him, but he didn't trust himself to walk her to the door.

Libby turned to him. "I'm glad I could tell you," she said and looked away, but back again. "I wish I could tell you more."

Her voice was soft, and Nick thought, *it would be so easy*

to lean into her, taste her lips. And so unprofessional and against everything he said he was about.

"Someday," he said, and he hoped there would be one.

Libby turned and opened the door. After she stepped out, she bent down and said, "Thank you, Nick."

"You're welcome, Libby."

He smiled as he watched her enter her building. She'd called him Nick.

CHAPTER 19

*L*ibby was relieved once Nick left the office. He'd be in Half Moon Bay visiting their newest project for the rest of the day. And it was Friday. Thank goodness it was Friday.

She needed a break from him, or rather her head, heart, and hormones did. Nick had become a Triple-H Threat.

Over the past few days since dinner, they worked efficiently and well together, but her thoughts would stray throughout the day, and she'd catch herself daydreaming about what it would be like if she could touch Nick again. Sometimes she fantasized about telling him that she was his Cinderella, only to be overcome with fear and shame for what the fallout might be. More and more, she was beginning to accept that she might need to resign sooner than later, and the idea of not seeing him five days a week made her heart ache. How had this happened?

And sometimes she caught him watching her too. Her heartbeat picked up each time, and she cautioned herself to think nothing of it and to stop thinking about him.

Absentmindedly, she picked up her desk phone. "Libby Duncan," she answered.

"Ms. Duncan, it's Luke Cooper."

A decision! "I'm sorry, Mr. Cooper, Mr. Tremaine is offsite this afternoon, but I can contact him and have him call you from his cell."

"I'm not looking for Tremaine. I need to speak to you."

She didn't hesitate. "You'll have to run this by our legal department first. I'm sure you can appreciate—"

"It's about your stepsister, Roxanne," he interrupted.

Libby gasped.

He reeled off his address. "Can you come to my office after work?"

After catching her breath, she said, "Yes."

Luke and Libby faced each other across his desk. Typically, his silence made people nervous, and they spoke first, but Ms. Duncan wasn't budging. If she was surprised to receive his call, she wasn't showing it now. Composed and calm, she appeared determined to wait him out.

A worthy component. Or maybe a comrade.

He explained, "I didn't know you knew Roxanne Blair until the night of the depositions."

She didn't respond.

"I asked Roxanne if she had any family she could turn to for support."

He had her attention now.

"She said no," he said.

Libby leaned forward, seemingly concerned. "Is she okay?"

Of course, she didn't know he'd told Roxanne she had no case.

"She will be. But she could use some support."

"Financial support?"

"Among other things," he said.

She shook her head as if to clear her head. "Her Aunt Grace is always there for her. I'm sorry, Mr. Cooper, but what is this about if not the deposition?"

"What has stopped you from telling him?"

She flinched.

His hunch was right: Nick had no idea Libby knew Roxanne.

Libby was done lying. "What I'm about to tell you, I'd like the opportunity to tell Nick first."

He nodded.

She told him the entire story—well, not about the gala and her wild attraction to Nick. She started from the beginning when she needed a job not only to support herself but for business research, how she'd learned about it from Grace, and the status of her business.

Luke rested his steepled fingertips against his lip as if he was contemplating what she had told him.

"What *does* he know?" he asked.

"That I'm building a side business, but not what the business is—"

"Why not?"

"It's not relevant and doesn't affect my performance at work."

"Okay, what does he know about Roxanne?"

"Everything except that I knew her a very long time ago."

"Why would you work for someone who has harassment claims against him?" Even Luke didn't believe Nick had harassed Roxanne, but Libby didn't know that.

"Because I knew Roxanne once. People don't change *that* much," she said.

Point taken, he thought.

She continued without prodding. "And working with Nick … As I told you before, nobody cares more about his employees than Nick Tremaine, and I can imagine, no, I believe, that Roxanne might have misinterpreted his attention, especially when it comes to his employees. Her mother married often, and, well, you get the picture."

Luke nodded. The saying *great minds think alike* came to mind, but he didn't share his thoughts.

"When's the last time you saw her?" he asked for confirmation.

"Not since we were children. What do you want, Mr. Cooper?"

He shook his head, unable to tell her where he stood on the case, but confident he hadn't misjudged the situation. The relationship between Roxanne and Libby had been a surprise, and it wasn't a coincidence, but it didn't change what he believed to be the truth about Nick Tremaine.

"Thank you for coming in. I won't mention our discussion to anyone. And for what it's worth, I think Roxanne could use a sister, or a friend, like you."

Libby squinted suspiciously at him. "You like her."

It wasn't a question, so he didn't answer. Instead, he

offered, "If things don't work out with Nick, and you need a job, call me."

Fortunately, Libby Duncan didn't seem insulted or tempted to slap him as Roxanne had done. She acknowledged his offer with a slight nod and left.

No two sisters, step or otherwise, could be less alike.

CHAPTER 20

a Monday had never been so full of surprises, at least not for Nick.

Libby had come to work without a bun. Over the weekend, she'd had her hair cut to a shoulder-length bob and dammit if she didn't look amazing. And he wasn't the only one pleased with the change. Male and female employees dropped by for no apparent reason to say "hi" to Libby and compliment her. In some ways, it was like seeing a new Libby. Not only because of her hair, but she carried herself differently too.

If he was honest with himself, and he was, he didn't think he could stay in the same room with her anymore if she made any other adjustments to her appearance, even though he'd been the one to encourage her to ditch the costume and blend in with the company culture. He recalled how she'd looked in his car after dinner, more relaxed with her jacket off and her blouse unbuttoned at the collar. He could imagine her bob sliding back and forth across her shoulders, getting caught in her loose collar, and him being tempted to run his fingers along the loose strands to brush them aside. Maybe he'd push aside her shirt's neckline as well ... *No. No. No.* He could barely handle the idea.

This was Beth's fault. If his phantom woman had left her number, he'd be spending more time with her than his imagination. He sent an email to his contact at the gala, Julie.

Sorry to be the pest, but do you have the gala attendee list?

She had replied, *Sorry. Been out of town on a family emergency. In touch soon.*

Nick was in the midst of one of the errant, this-is-a-bad-idea Libby fantasies when Lukas Cooper called to say Nick's legal team could expect an email shortly. He thanked Nick for his time and said, "I'm dropping the case." If Nick weren't so wound up about Beth and Libby, relief and exhaustion would have overcome him.

Jim and Melissa arrived at his office shortly after, and he heard Melissa say, "Libby, join us. You'll want to hear this."

Oh, lord help him. He hoped Libby sat across the room from him. The irony that Lukas was ending the case while Nick had the hots for his new assistant and couldn't be in the same room was too much. He needed a vacation for more reasons than one.

Libby followed Melissa and Jim into Nick's office. One of two things was about to happen. She had recognized

Lukas Cooper's number when he rang Nick's office. Nick had picked up the call before she could. There was either good news about Roxanne's suit, or they were all there to fire Libby, though she had a hard time believing Lukas Cooper had gone against his word to keep her confidence.

Nick looked at her but glanced away quickly. He hadn't said a thing about her haircut, and she was partly happy that he didn't make a big deal about it while also piqued that he didn't seem impressed. She was angry with herself for caring. When she'd shown up to the salon, she'd intended to get the usual trim and highlights, but instead, she'd seen a young woman with a sassy bob leaving, and she'd realized she was desperate for some sort of change. She was tired of being a wallflower. But caring if her boss noticed or not? She was worse than Roxanne. As if Nick noticed her at all.

"Take a seat team. Lukas Cooper just called me warning me he'd be in touch. What's the scoop?" Of course, he knew, but they deserved this moment. It was their quality work that had cleared his name, not Cooper.

"Not only has Lukas Cooper dropped out, but he has also convinced Roxanne Blair that she has no case. Ever. It's over, Nick," Jim said.

Nick smiled and walked around the desk to clasp Jim's hand and then pull him into a hug. As soon as they stopped pounding each other's backs, Melissa hugged Nick.

"Finally," Melissa said.

Nick turned, and there was Libby. Without thinking, he pulled her into a professional embrace. It only took a nanosecond to regret his decision. Both jumped back as if burned. Fortunately, Jim and Melissa were hugging each other and missed their reactions.

Nick moved back to the other side of the desk.

Libby's eyes were wide, and she said, "Congratulations, Nick. I think I hear someone in the outer office." And she retreated as fast as possible.

Libby returned to her desk only after visiting the restroom and splashing cold water on her face. She had it bad. She couldn't keep working closely with Nick. She also couldn't keep living on the edge, wondering when he'd learn the truth. She needed to resign so she could be honest with him. And at least then, he'd never know she'd grown so attracted to him and liked him much more than an assistant should like her boss.

And now was the time too. Financially, it wasn't the best, but she had savings. It would be awkward to take Lukas Cooper up on his offer, but it was good to know it was there. She could always temp during the day for an agency. Now that Roxanne was done and wouldn't be filing further claims, it would be easier for Nick to find a replacement without the charges looming over him and the company. *Yes,* Libby decided, *I need to give my notice.* And at some point, she could be honest with Nick, maybe even about the gala.

She knew from Dana that Connor had, not too subtly, repeatedly asked for her partner's full name. It was clear to Libby that Nick was still thinking about the gala, not his assistant.

Staying in this office, the proximity, and being crazy attracted to him wasn't going to do anyone any favors—especially her, since the feelings were unrequited.

That night, she handed him her notice, and Nick announced he was going on vacation.

CHAPTER 21

Ah, the value of vacation. Nick had missed the office. He loved his work and returning to it after a week away gave him great pleasure. If only he could put off what was to come: confirmation that Libby was still resigning.

The vacation had been a healthy decision. The distance from Roxanne's accusations as well as the space from Libby and his inexplicable attraction to her, had brought great perspective.

He liked Libby. And if she left by her own choice and for all the right reasons, such as her following her dreams, then in time, he could ask her on a date. She might say no, but he would try.

He'd gained perspective on Beth too. For whatever reason, the woman hadn't wanted to hear from him. There could be any number of reasons. Who knew who she was as a person, or what was going on in her life? Not him. He was letting the fantasy go and focusing on a chance with

Libby. There was something there between them. He hoped he wasn't imagining it.

Now, all he had to do was get through one week with her. At one point, he thought it might be possible he'd see her after vacation and not react, but he knew himself well enough to be certain that he felt something for her. What and how much, he wasn't sure, but his reaction to her was unusual for him. Sure, he'd dated and often, but these days he constantly thought about Libby, and that was the difference.

Instead of being nervous to see her, he was looking forward to it. He hoped she secretly felt the same.

"Nick?"

Ah, she was here. Since dinner, they'd stayed on a first-name basis, another change he'd taken great pains not to bring attention to. He turned to her and smiled, unable to keep the the pleasure of seeing her from his face. His chest constricted a bit, and he hoped someday soon he'd be able to greet her by taking her into his arms. After hugging her last week, he knew just where her head would rest against his chest, how far he'd have to dip to kiss her … *Stop.*

She smiled, too, and yes, that was a blush he saw. Yes, she was happy to see him too. Someday, he'd be able to say he missed her, but for now, he said, "Hi."

"Hi," she said. "How was your time off?"

"Much needed. How was the office?" He really wanted to ask how was she.

"Very good. I've been training my replacement. You know Burt from accounting? We hired internally."

"Melissa called me and told me. Excellent decision," he said. He sat down at his desk in case his body decided to show her how much he liked her bob and the pink cashmere sweater that had replaced her starched shirt and jacket. "So you're still leaving."

"I'm still leaving." She approached his desk and sat down.

"Business is going well," he said, not really asking.

"It's too soon to say, but our open house is this Friday night and the RSVPs are solid. I need to focus. I can't be a part-time business owner."

Nick nodded. "And the business is …?"

"Not ready to tell you yet," she said.

He didn't press her. "The offer stands. Always ready to help," he said. *In as many ways as possible.*

"Thank you."

"One week left, then. What's our schedule look like?"

"Burt will be here in a moment and the three of us can go over it together."

Libby had to last only five more days—four and a three quarters now. Since they'd hired internally, training was moving quickly. Having a third person around would be good for Libby's control, or lack thereof.

She had missed Nick. She was so stupid happy to see him. And for a brief minute when she first saw him, she thought he might have missed her in some strange way too. But perhaps it had been her imagination. Less than a week from now, she would tell him the truth. She had already decided she'd tell him everything no matter what, but it would have to wait until she wasn't an employee and after the Seconds Impressions open house on Friday night.

~

Four days later, Nick was crawling out of his skin. He should have taken two weeks off. Acknowledging his interest in Libby while having to pretend he didn't feel anything was making him climb the walls. He'd taken steps to alleviate the tension—tension he wasn't even sure Libby noticed, she was so busy training Burt. A few times, he caught her daydreaming, most likely about her new company. He knew what it felt like to be excited about one's work. Every chance he had, he moved a meeting to a boardroom or to a team member's office rather than his, just to create some distance. He'd even taken a lunch break all week, just to get outside and walk off some of the heightened sensitivity. Damn, but he couldn't wait to take a risk and ask her out. To kiss her ... if she said yes, of course.

He was sure there was something there, but then again, he'd thought he and Beth had a combustible connection. Obviously, Beth had not.

For the last few days, Nick had watched Libby at the bus line. She no longer had hair to let down so there was no end-of-day transition. Except each day, she turned, looked up, and smiled. He never mentioned it. Neither did she. It was their secret. He hoped he was right about the meaning. He couldn't say anything as long as she was employed at Tremaine Development.

Now, he watched the clock. What was the saying about watched pots never boiling? The same applied to clocks and passing time. He'd told Burt, his new assistant, to not plan anything past four p.m. He'd gone to Libby's going away party, pretended the cake didn't taste like sawdust in his mouth, and had spoken to the attendees, praising Libby's contributions to the company. All true.

But at five o'clock when she was ready to leave, he was walking her out.

Here we go. It was five o'clock sharp. He grabbed his briefcase and jacket and surprised Burt and Libby with his punctual departure.

"Libby, I'll walk you out."

Libby hadn't expected time alone with Nick before she officially left. All week her fingers had itched to touch him and see if he felt anything for her. When they reached the elevator, she was grateful no one joined them; she only had four floors of Nick to herself. Who knew when she'd get a chance to see him again. Even as excited as she was to be starting her own business, she struggled with the idea of not seeing him every day. The idea that he could forget about her as soon as she left squeezed her heart. She had to know if there was something between them. She didn't want to regret never saying anything, not taking the risk.

They both started talking at the same time.

"Nick, I like you."

"Can I call you?"

As their words registered, the energy shifted. They both dropped their bags and met in the middle of the elevator, clutching each other as their lips came together. Libby wasted no time, she all but climbed up him until her lips could find his, the force of her passion pushing him against the elevator wall. Nick turned his mouth on hers to plunge his tongue deeply, and he reveled in the feel of her tongue sliding against his. They both groaned. He shoved his hands into her bob to cup her head, and she palmed his neck to hold his mouth hard against hers. When the elevator dinged, announcing their arrival, they jumped apart.

Nick grabbed his briefcase to hide his body's reaction from the lobby-goers, and Libby tried to smooth her hair. They both cleared their throats as they exited the elevator. It was a good thing Libby didn't wear lipstick because they'd both look like clowns.

"Good night, Mr. Tremaine," the receptionist called. "We will miss you, Libby."

Nick nodded, not trusting his voice.

The doorman held the door, "Mr. Tremaine. Ms. Duncan."

Once they were out of the doorman's earshot, Nick asked, "So I take it that was a yes?"

She smiled up at him. "Most definitely." She hoped he wouldn't take too long to call her.

"Good luck tonight. Remember to have fun," he said. If not for her new business's open house, he'd ask her out for dinner tonight. He was that anxious to get to know her on a different level. And to touch her again. "Can I give you a ride?"

She laughed throatily.

Nick's eyes darkened.

"I think I need some space to compose myself. The bus will set me straight."

"Putting business first. I like it," he joked. "I will call you."

The commitment in his voice, sent goosebumps over Libby's body. The good kind.

Her body still tingling from their electric kiss, Libby walked away. Nick was into her. Her! She looked over her shoulder. He was standing there, his eyes following her every step.

She hadn't been the only one experiencing the insane feelings, that explosive kiss proved it. A small voice inside said, *He didn't recognize you as Beth,* making her wonder, briefly, if he kissed all women like that. But she dismissed it. It was insane to be jealous of herself. There was no faking the intense connection. Both times.

Nick would call her. And when he did, she'd invite him to her place so she could tell him everything. The best place to start, other than that kiss, was with the truth. It was a risk, but they were worth it.

CHAPTER 22

*N*ick's Apple Watch rang as he ran the last mile to his house. After he and Libby parted ways, he'd gone for a run as soon as he got home. Grateful for hands-free technology, he glanced at the screen before taking the call: CONNOR.

"Connor," Nick said between breaths.

"Nick, what are you doing tonight?"

"No plans. Why?"

"I know where Beth will be."

When Nick didn't respond immediately, Connor said, "With Dana."

Nick almost laughed. "Thanks, Connor, but I'm letting all that go." *Libby is my priority.* He wasn't ready to explain this to Connor.

"Okay," Connor said, unfazed, unquestioning, and disconnected.

He walked the final quarter mile to cool off. His phone rang again. JULIE. *The gala list.* He hesitated. Two phone calls. Two people ready to point him in Beth's direction.

Ironic. But he no longer cared. But he should at least talk to Julie, ask her if her family was okay, and thank her for her time.

"It was my mother, but she's okay now. Thank you for asking," Julie said. "I have that list in front of me. What are you looking for?"

He hated to waste her time, so he said, "Seconds Impressions. Two attendees." Though he wouldn't be following up on the information.

"Found them," she said. "Dana Ross."

Yep, no surprise there.

"And Elizabeth Duncan."

Nick almost tripped on his doorstep. "Come again?"

"Dana Ross and Elizabeth Duncan," she confirmed.

Nick couldn't remember the rest of the discussion. From her personnel file, he knew Libby's full name. He paced his living room, torn between fury and humility.

Beth was Libby. Libby was Beth. And he'd had no fucking idea.

But Libby had.

He spoke to Siri on his watch. "Siri, call Connor."

"We just talked," Connor answered.

"When and where?" Nick asked.

"I thought you were letting that go," Connor said.

"I changed my mind."

Two hours later, Nick followed Connor into the bar and Seconds Impressions' reception. The hostess asked for their names as she reviewed a list. Connor gave his name and then said, "Nick's with me," as if the hostess didn't need to know anything else.

Nick spotted Libby immediately. She was in a black cocktail dress and looked stunning. Her bob teased her bare shoulders. Her lipstick-covered lips smiled widely as she spoke to two attendees. Dana approached her and whispered something in her ear, and Libby's smile grew broader—good news, apparently.

Nick followed Connor to the private bar for a drink but continued to watch Libby-Beth-Elizabeth. He'd never been more livid than he had earlier tonight, but that was personal. Right now, Libby was here for professional reasons. As upset as he was, he had no intention of interfering with her business or success tonight. What they had to discuss would be done alone and when he had her full attention. Which meant making sure she didn't see him now. If she did, she'd know he knew, and her attention to her clients would be screwed.

Gritting his teeth, he took his drink from Connor and said, "I'll explain later. Don't tell Dana I'm here. I'll call you tomorrow."

"We just got here ..." Connor said perplexed.

Nick followed a hall to a partially concealed and private lounge area adjacent to Libby's event. He'd wait here until the event was over.

Libby stepped to one side to survey the room. A full house. The night had been a smashing success. Periodically, Dana would check their website to see how many people had signed up for the next phase: the interviews. Over two hundred attendees tonight, and already they had almost one hundred clients. The crowd was starting to disperse.

Dana came to her, "Now that it's calming down, I'm going to say hi to Connor. And I'll get us a bottle of champagne to celebrate our super extra successful night!"

"I'll be over soon," Libby said. "I'll let the staff know we're wrapping up." Gratified and running on adrenaline not only from the night, but the embrace with Nick earlier, Libby was ready for a glass of champagne. She briefly wished Nick already knew all her secrets so he could be there with her, Dana, and his friend Connor for a toast. But when he called, and if he gave her a chance to explain, such a toast would be in their future.

But first things first, she had an event to wrap up. She went in search of the manager to give him the thumbs-up. Her high heels clapped against the tinted concrete floor as she walked down the hallway that connected the private room to the main restaurant, and then she collided with someone pacing the lounge.

She gasped and reached to steady herself. A strong, familiar hand found her hip. Shocked, she looked up into Nick's irate face.

She jumped back. "Nick! What are you doing here?" But she knew. He'd found her out before she could tell him herself.

He shook his head. "Surprised, Elizabeth? Or should I say Dana?"

She paled. "I can explain," she said taking a step backward.

He followed her until she was literally backed into the

corner. He stopped inches before her and put one hand against the wall beside her head. "Are your customers gone?"

She nodded.

"Good," he said. "Start explaining, but first ..." He swooped in and pressed his lips firmly against hers.

She opened her mouth wide and invited him in.

The kiss seemed to carry on forever, but it could only have been seconds.

Shoes slapped against the hallway floor announcing an interruption.

Nick tore his lips from hers and rested his forehead on the cool wall above her head.

She was disoriented from his sudden appearance, hot kiss, and the warmth of his body and his cologne swirling around her.

Once the unknown person passed, Libby huskily said, "I was going to tell you everything when you called me. I planned to invite you to my house so we could talk."

He groaned and stepped back. Only moments ago, Nick was convinced he'd been played a fool and that Libby had been laughing at him for weeks. For a brief minute, he'd even wondered if her lies had something to do with Roxanne Blair but had rejected the idea since the case was dismissed. Now, he wanted to hear her out and believe her. He hadn't planned to kiss her again; he'd been unable to stop himself from touching and tasting what he believed to be the truth. Their reaction to each other couldn't be faked. He'd known enough women to know better.

An inner voice reminded him, *You weren't supposed to be at the gala. She was hiding on the balcony. Dana tried to stop you* ... Nick ran his hand through is hair and then looked at Libby. "We're settling this tonight. I'll wait at the bar until you're ready to go." He pulled a clean hanky from his pocket, and gently reached over to fix her lipstick, and then he roughly wiped his face.

"Perfect," she said. "I will find you."

Dana and Connor looked stunned as Libby approached them. Nick was ready and waiting. Connor said, "Aren't you ..."

"My former assistant?" Nick asked. "Yes."

Nick put out his hand, and Libby settled hers within. "Ready?" he asked, but he didn't wait for her to answer. He'd already collected their coats and he draped hers over her shoulders. "Connor. Dana," he said by way of goodbye.

Dana's eyes were popping from her head. "I'll call you tomorrow, Dana," Libby said. If Nick didn't kill her or break her heart. "Goodnight, Connor."

They were silent on their way to Libby's apartment. She hadn't even thought to ask him where they would go to talk, but she was glad it was her place. He'd probably storm out when he heard the truth now.

Nick looked around, surprised but not surprised by Libby's loft. It didn't suit Ms. Duncan, but he suspected it suited Libby. The one he hoped to know better.

Libby took his jacket while he loosened his tie. She kicked off her high heels and they stared at each other from the center of her living room.

What now? Libby wondered. *Where do we start? How do we start?*

"I'm sorry," she said.

He shook his head. "That's the worst thing you could say."

"I wanted to tell you," she said.

"Getting better," he said.

"You weren't supposed to be at the gala, and the kiss. That kiss …" She paused.

Nick only stared. He put his hands on his hips, waiting her out. What he needed her to say, wanted her to say, was that he hadn't imagined the chemistry. That it hadn't been one-sided. That she hadn't felt like she had to do what she did to protect her identity.

"… blew me away," she finished.

His voice was husky. "Even better."

Tears of frustration pooled in her eyes. "And I didn't want to ruin the moment. You felt so good. So damn good …"

And he forgave her right then and there. Two steps and he had her in his arms again.

Lips inches apart, their breaths bounced off each other, and she said, "Wait, Nick. There's more."

But it was too late for talking. They were lost. Unlike their other kisses, Nick's lips caressed hers slowly. She sighed and opened her lips. His tongue slid sensually inside, and a groan vibrated up his core and against her.

He slid her skirt up and lifted her against him. She moaned and wrapped her legs around his waist. He stopped kissing her long enough to stare into her eyes. "I haven't been able to stop thinking of you. Both of you. All of you."

"Me either," she said and kissed him. "To the bed, please." She unlocked her legs from his waist to slide her feet to the floor.

Groaning, he said, "Lead the way."

After a few short steps to her bedroom loft, they undressed before each other and fell on to the bed in a tangle of passion and intensity. An urgency overtook them. Libby grabbed one of the condoms from the nightstand that she'd bought earlier. "I bought these for us," she said. "I had hoped someday …"

He pulled her back beside him and rolled on top of her. "Let me show you my thanks," he said and started to kiss his way down her body.

"Later," she said. "Please."

Nick didn't need to be asked twice. "Many laters," he confirmed as he unwrapped the protection. He slid on top of her, deep inside of her, and then and there, he fell.

CHAPTER 23

*L*ibby rolled on top of Nick's naked body, the sheets a messy pile at the foot of the bed. "Maybe I don't want you to get up or dressed."

Nick chuckled as he stared up into her horny eyes. "Who said anything about getting dressed?" He slid his hand from her shoulder down to the upward swell of her behind and repeated the journey. Back and forth. Back and forth. "You're going to kill me, you know."

"I've only just begun," she said and sighed.

He placed his hands on either side of her face and gave her a long tender kiss. She leaned into his embrace. When it ended, she hid her face in the curve of his strong neck. "Nick?"

"Hmm." His hand stroked the small of her back.

It was time to tell him about Roxanne. Her heart sped up. She slid her arms under his shoulders and nestled her face further into his neck to anchor herself and to hold onto him as tight as she could. She didn't want to lose him. "I want to tell you—"

The doorbell rang, and she groaned. *Now?* When she was finally ready to tell him? She would ignore it. It was probably an Amazon delivery or something. She wasn't expecting anyone. Nick and the truth were her priority.

"Saved by the bell," he joked, reminding her of the same words she'd spoken to him at the gala when Connor had called him.

He placed his hands on her waist and lifted her off him. "I'll jump in the shower. You know where to find me once you've taken care of the visitor."

She threw on her robe and ran toward the front door. She'd barely had a chance to open it before Roxanne pushed her way through.

Roxanne took in Libby's tumbled hair and robe. "My, isn't this just perfect."

Horror washed over Libby. "What are you doing here? How did you get my address?"

"Grace. Luke. Lots of resources."

"You're not welcome here, Roxanne. You need to leave. Now." Libby glanced quickly over her shoulder. *Damn. Damn. Damn.* She prayed Nick was already in the bathroom. This was not the way things were supposed to happen!

Roxanne looked around the front room and must have seen Nick's jacket draped across the back of the couch. "I see you aren't alone. Goody. This will only take a few minutes." Roxanne pushed her way farther inside.

"Libby, where is—" Nick leaned over the loft railing and froze. "What in the hell? Libby get away from her." Wrapped only in a towel, he took the stairs two at a time.

He stepped past Roxanne and pulled Libby safely

behind him. "Get out of here before I call the police. Are you stalking me now?"

Roxanne looked at her chipped nails and laughed. "Nick, don't be so dramatic. I just had some information I would like to share with you. Libby and I are well acquainted. Aren't we, sis? I like what you've done with the place."

Nick tensed and looked over his shoulder at Libby. *Sis?*

Libby stepped around him as if to shield him from Roxanne instead. "Get out of here Roxanne," she said.

Roxanne laughed again. "We never did care for each other. But soon, we'll be sitting at the same table in the courthouse. Isn't that so, Libs? Now that you've told Luke."

A sense of dread was viciously winding its way through Nick, turning his blood cold. "Libby?" he asked between clenched teeth.

Libby was furious at Roxanne and scared of Nick's reaction. "Roxanne, I don't know what you are up to, but it will not work. You and I both know the case was dismissed."

Nick froze and stepped away from Libby. "You *do* know her."

Roxanne leaned forward and brushed a nail down his naked chest.

Libby swatted her hand away.

"Let me explain the situation to you, dear Nicky. Libby is my sister and after the injustice you delivered, she agreed to become your assistant to gain evidence for my case."

"Never," Libby yelled.

Roxanne continued. "The case is far from being dismissed, Nick. Thanks to Libby, it's stronger than ever."

Nick roared and whirled toward Libby.

Libby paled. Her hand fluttered to her neck. "Nick, you know not to believe her."

Roxanne clapped her hands together and glided toward the door. "I hope the two of you have a beautiful day."

Libby turned toward Nick.

He stood with his back to her and his hands clenched at his hips. He rolled his head from one side and then the other. The muscles of his back rippled with tension.

"Nick, this is what I wanted to tell you last night. To explain about Roxanne." She stood and touched his back.

He turned on her and she stepped back at the warning in his eyes. He walked up the stairs with icy control.

She followed him.

"Stay away from me, Libby." He started yanking his clothes on. His hands punched through the sleeves of his shirt. While he jerkily buttoned his shirt, he stared at her with accusation. Shirt untucked, he sat on the bed to jerk on his socks.

She sank to the bed to sit next to him. "I can explain."

"Don't fucking bother. It's been one lie after another." He walked down the stairs. The possibility of explosion following in his wake. He grabbed his jacket and then his keys off the side table.

He yanked at the door.

"Nick!" she yelled.

The door slammed and the finality reverberated through the walls.

CHAPTER 24

Roxanne sat in her car, waiting for Nick to leave Libby's apartment. When he did, she thought she might get sick with shame.

After slamming Libby's door, he leaned against it and covered his eyes with one hand before swiping it through his hair. He walked to his car, disheveled, dazed, and confused. Before climbing in, he looked across the roof toward Libby's apartment.

And from where Roxanne sat, the man looked crushed. There was no other way for Roxanne to describe it. And it didn't feel right to make anyone, including Nick, look like or feel devastated. She'd been betrayed and hurt before.

Who had she become? The truth was ugly: her bitter, man-hating mother.

When Nick drove away, Roxanne climbed out of her car and approached Libby's apartment, her energy and resentment gone. Shame made her shoulders drop.

Roxanne only hated herself more when she knocked,

and Libby flung open the door with a look of heart-wrenching hope and love for Nick.

Helplessly, Roxanne said, "He's gone."

Libby glared at her. "Please leave, Roxanne. You've done all the damage you could do."

"I'll fix it," Roxanne said. "I will."

"You can't," Libby said sadly and closed the door.

Roxanne stumbled back to her car. She'd always been too emotional for her own good. Why didn't she learn? What had even possessed her to drive over to Libby's and confront her?

Aunt Grace.

Kicked out of her apartment, Roxanne had been unpacking her suitcase in Grace's guest room. Grace had listened while Roxanne cried through her baggage, literally and figuratively.

"And then," she told her beloved aunt, "I found out that Libby took my job with Nick! Can you believe it?"

And from the lack of surprise on her aunt's face, Roxanne knew that yes, her aunt certainly could believe it. Just one more person who had betrayed her. Libby was ruining everything for her. Unable to sleep all night, as soon day broke, she'd found Libby's address—her aunt still kept a Rolodex, of all things—and raced to her apartment.

Would she have gone if she'd known Nick would be there? She'd never know.

Wiping her tears of guilt, Roxanne dialed Luke's number.

"Roxanne?" he asked, surprised. "Are you okay?"

"No. I messed up. I need help fixing it." She told him what she had done, including how she'd found out about

Libby by reading his file. For what could have only been seconds but felt like hours, Luke said nothing.

In the end, she wished he wouldn't have said anything at all.

"The only thing you can fix is yourself," he said and hung up.

CHAPTER 25

*L*ibby and Dana high-fived. Their afternoon round of timed dates had gone super-duper. Or like "awesome sauce," as Dana had put it.

Libby wished she was feeling like awesome sauce. The business was going better than expected, but it had been three weeks since she'd seen or heard from Nick. She'd tried to call him, but when he couldn't be bothered to return her calls, she refused to grovel. She'd said she had something important to tell him. They'd both chosen sex first. Perhaps that's where they'd always gone wrong. Their insane sexual chemistry had taken precedence, and like most explosive things, they had exploded before they'd even tried to make anything work.

Funnily enough, Luke Cooper had become a friend, of sorts, and a client. She wondered if he'd left yet. While he'd been charming and drawn lots of attention from the other guests today, Libby didn't think he would pursue any of the minutes-long dates. Maybe next time.

Luke told her about Roxanne's confession. While she

had tried to shrug off his friendly concern, he said, "He'll come around. He's not an idiot. See you next time. Good job."

She shook her head. *Enough of Nick. Moving on. Go home. Go for a run.* She was signing the bill when the object of her desire entered the restaurant with a drop-dead gorgeous woman. The manager was all but tripping over himself to get to Nick's companion, for some reason. Maybe Nick and his date were regulars.

Nick saw her and froze as their eyes met across the bar.

The hostess was walking away. Nick's pretty companion said, "Nicky."

Nicky. Libby looked away, handed the ticket to the bartender, and grabbed her jacket. Nick had ignored her calls, making it clear there was nothing personal to pursue, not even a friendship. And he hadn't wasted any time meeting someone else.

"Nicky," his date called again.

"I'll be there in a minute," he said, not looking away from Libby.

Since he stood in her path to the door, she lifted her chin and approached him. "Hello, Nicky," Libby said, trying for some levity.

Though his jaw was tight, she thought he'd been tempted to smile.

"Libby," he said. He looked over her shoulder. "Another event?"

"Yes," she said.

"Going well?"

"Very well."

"I'm glad," he said, and she believed him. He might not

like her as a person anymore, but he'd always liked seeing new business owners succeed.

"Well, I need to get going," Libby said just before his date called his name again. "And apparently, so do you." She moved to step around him.

He reached out and cupped her elbow to stop her. His eyes widened, and he dropped his hand to his side and clenched his fist.

He began, "I should have called—"

"You don't need to explain," she interrupted. "I hurt you, and I'm sorrier than you know. Goodbye, Mr. Tremaine," she said for good measure. This time, she took a wide step to the side, walked past him, and out the door. She didn't look back.

CHAPTER 26

*W*ho was that, Nicky?" his aunt asked as soon as he took a seat. His mother's youngest sister was a successful author and his age. He and Natalie had grown up together, more like siblings—even more so than his mother and Natalie. He should leave, chase after Libby. Tell her he couldn't stop thinking about her. He'd been trying to figure out how to approach her and apologize, since last Friday, ever since Melissa Bancroft had left his office, asking him off the cuff, "By the way, did you ever find out how Libby Duncan knew Roxanne Blair?"

Stunned, and immediately feeling nauseous, he'd asked her, "What?" Nick hadn't told *anyone* that Libby and Roxanne knew each other. No one.

Melissa had wrinkled her nose and said, "Right. I never told you, and I guess Libby didn't either, but they knew each other many years ago. Libby said it had been decades since they'd been in touch."

He'd been a complete fucking idiot.

No matter what had happened, he needed to see Libby again and apologize for his actions. She had tried to tell him. They'd been so busy falling into bed, he hadn't given her a chance.

Fortunately, he didn't have to answer Natalie, because someone stepped up to their table.

"Hello, Tremaine."

Nick was surprised to see Lukas Cooper. All these years in the same city, and he'd never run into him once. He stood and shook Cooper's hand. "Cooper."

"And who is this?" Natalie all but purred.

After making introductions, Luke peered at Nick. Luke wasn't interested in Nick's "aunt," or in anyone for that matter, except the one person he shouldn't think about at all: Roxanne.

Both showing support for Libby's new venture and feeling like shit that Roxanne had found Libby because of him, Luke had signed up for Seconds Impressions.

Luke hiked his thumb over his shoulder. "You just missed Libby."

Nick tensed. "I didn't realize you knew each other so well."

"I'm a customer," Luke said, smiling smugly.

Nick raised his brows. "Seriously?"

"Sure, why not," and then Luke went in for the kill. He'd always liked to stir the pot. "Now, if only I can persuade *her* to go on a date."

Tremaine's brows crashed into a frown.

Yeah, Tremaine didn't like that. "I'll leave the two of you alone," Luke said. "By the way, I'm sorry about Roxanne. For what it's worth, before Roxanne showed up at Libby's, Libby hadn't seen her in more than twenty years. They were stepsisters for a brief time. That's it."

CHAPTER 27

*L*ibby had a sick feeling in her stomach that her godmother was up to something.

Grace had called her and said she was heading to Libby's loft now. She needed help deciphering an insurance claim or something or other. Since Grace was on the OCD spectrum, the urgency wasn't unheard of, though Libby wished that today of all days she could put her off. Seeing Nick yesterday had taken the wind out of her sails, and she needed to break the spell and get motivated for another dating round tonight at a posh restaurant.

When she opened the front door, Grace said, "Just hear her out."

"Who?"

"Me," Roxanne said, stepping into the doorway.

"Not now. Not ever," Libby said. What was she supposed to do now? She couldn't slam the door in Grace's face too.

"I'm sorry, Libby. I want to make amends."

Amends, right. And yet, Libby hesitated. It would have meant the world to Libby if Nick had at least let her apologize and let *her* make amends. And she recalled Luke Cooper's words that he thought Roxanne could use a friend like Libby. "Come in." She stepped aside so the women could enter.

Grace hugged Libby. "Thanks, sweetie."

"Anytime," Libby said facetiously and waved them toward the sofa.

Roxanne leaned forward earnestly, "Libby, I'm sorry for hurting you and for hurting Nick. I didn't know he was here, and when I saw him, I just lost it. Wait. I want to do this right. The truth is, I lost it before I came over, or I would have stopped myself from hurting you. If I could fix it, I would."

Libby nodded. There was no point in dissecting Roxanne's words or choices. "Thank you for apologizing."

There was an awkward silence. Grace said, "Roxanne is volunteering now."

"Really?" Libby asked. "Which organization?"

"It's for young women who have aged out of the foster system," Roxanne said.

Libby couldn't ignore the spark in Roxanne's eyes nor the proud lift of her chin. "Tell me more about it."

By the time Roxanne finished, Libby knew how to respond. "Excuse me for a minute." Libby returned with the suits she'd worn as Ms. Duncan, all freshly dry-cleaned. She held the hangers out to Roxanne, who stood up, puzzled.

"What's this about?"

Libby smiled. "Please take these clothes. Give them to

your ladies for interviews. Feel free to alter them. Use them however they will support your purpose."

Tears rushed to Roxanne's eyes. She said, "Yes, my purpose. Thank you, Libby."

As Grace and Roxanne walked out, Libby couldn't help but smile when she heard Roxanne repeat to Grace, "I have a purpose."

CHAPTER 28

*L*ibby and Dana put the final touches on the dating tables. "I don't want to participate," Libby said.

"You have to because we have an odd number of participants, and I'm seeing Connor. I can't pretend to be dating."

"But I'm one of the owners. Is this ethical?"

"We'll iron out this kink, so it won't happen again, but for now it's too late. You're single. You *should* be dating."

"Not now, Dana, please. I will when I'm ready."

"What are we going to do? Let someone sit alone for three minutes? We can't."

Libby sighed with frustration. "You're right. And if I can't be convinced to try our service, why am I asking people to trust us?"

"Exactly," Dana said. "Here, I brought a dress for you."

Libby looked at the suit she had on. "What's wrong with what I'm wearing?"

"Just try it on," Dana said. "It's better for a date."

"Dates," Libby corrected. "Plural." They had twenty men and nineteen women tonight, twenty counting her.

"I'll finish up here," Dana said as guests started arriving. "Go change."

～

Libby stared at herself in the mirror. Dana's dress did look great on her. One shoulder was bare, and her now wedged bob brushed one collar bone. She added some lipstick. *Voila.* Ready to pretend she was interested in dating anyone other than Nick. *Lights. Camera. Action.*

When she opened the door, Dana was waiting for her, and she looked uncharacteristically nervous. "You look smashing," Dana said.

"Thank you. I love the dress," Libby said. "Why are you waiting for me? Why aren't you greeting our guests?"

"Connor is helping."

Oh, oh. Libby turned to race to the main room before Connor said or did the wrong thing as he was apt to do, lacking a few filters. Personally, she found his honesty refreshing, and obviously, Dana did too, but some of their guests might not.

She'd only taken one step when Dana cupped her shoulders from behind and turned her one hundred eighty degrees. "Your date is in there."

There was a cozy room to the side of their privately reserved space. Libby had used it in the past to store their supplies or to catch a breath. "What? Why did we set up one table so far removed?"

Dana nudged her forward and said, "I'll check on everyone else."

This makes no sense. She'd fix this right away. Planning to take her date to the main room, Libby stepped confidently inside only to lose her breath.

Nick.

Heart pounding in her ears, she took in his splendor. He was a sight for sore eyes.

The candlelit table was set for two. Music played in the background, and he was holding dozens of roses.

"Libby, will you have dinner with me?"

"What are you doing here?

"I came to apologize."

"A call would have been sufficient," she said in her best Ms. Duncan voice.

"That wouldn't have been good enough. And besides, you probably wouldn't have taken my call."

"I tried to call you," she said.

"I'm sorry."

She swallowed.

"I'm sorry," he said again.

She nodded, clearing her throat. "I'm sorry too. I didn't know Roxanne anymore ..."

"I believe you."

"Why now?"

He clenched his jaw.

Someone had vouched for her. "Who?" she asked. "Who gave you confidence in me?"

"I was getting there on my own," he said.

"But how did you get there *completely*?"

"Cooper, but he isn't the reason I'm here. Libby, I can't

stop thinking about you. I made mistakes; the biggest one was walking away." He set the roses on the table and took a step toward her.

She looked up. "I should have told you sooner."

"Shall we start again? This time on a real date, like a normal couple?"

"Nick, this is hardly a normal date."

"But it's the first of many to come, I promise." He pulled out her chair. "Please have dinner with me."

Being near him again was exquisite. Libby desperately wanted to pinch herself. There was one other thing she needed to know before she could risk her heart again. "What about the woman I saw you with?"

For a second, he seemed confused, but then his eyes lit up and then darkened with intensity. "My Aunt Natalie, hence the nickname, Nicky. She is my mom's youngest sister. Long story."

"Ah, the author," she said.

"Yes." Nick caressed her cheek. "You are the only woman for me, Libby." He extended his hand. "Take my hand, and I'm yours forever, Cinderella."

She placed her hand in his. He turned her hand up and kissed her palm. "Here's to a new beginning," he said.

"Here's to *beginning*," she said and smiled.

And so they began their life together.

EPILOGUE

$\mathcal{N}$ow for the last board meeting agenda item regarding Aging Out & Onward," the chairman said. "Loretta made the case for an additional headcount. The role would be Social Coordinator and responsibilities would include mentoring our residents for interviews, social etiquette, communication skills, business writing, college and trade school visits, guest speakers, and administrative assistance as needed."

The directors asked multiple questions, clarifying that the role would help empower women, offering independence and resourcefulness. Loretta, the house manager, spoke up, reassuring everyone that a volunteer had already implemented the program without spending a penny, and the results spoke for themselves. In the past three months, the volunteer mentor had helped one student begin cosmetology school, a second gained admittance to the university social work program, and a third was training to become an EMT. And that wasn't all. The same person had coordinated a professional clothing drive, so the girls had professional attire for their interviews. The list went on.

"Loretta, if you'll excuse us."

As soon as she left, the chairman said, "Let's put it to a vote."

The role was approved, and the quarterly meeting was called to an end.

After saying goodbye to his peers, Luke hung back and found Loretta. "I'd like to meet this person who has made such a difference."

For a second, he thought Loretta looked confused, but then she said, "Follow me. She's out in the herb garden."

"When did we start a garden?" he asked. "Don't tell me. This is also thanks to the same person."

They reached the door leading to the back yard. Loretta stepped aside and waved him through. "I don't think introductions will be necessary."

Luke frowned and followed her pointed look. Wearing a bright red sun hat, jeans, and a T-shirt was the one and only Roxanne Blair.

Stunned, Luke asked Loretta, "Roxanne has been here the entire time?"

"Yep, ever since you sent her over months ago. I thought you knew."

No. He'd tried to call her once, but she never called back. He went by her apartment, and she had moved. He figured his tough love had gone too far, but maybe not.

"Roxanne, there's someone here to see you," Loretta called and then left.

He sauntered across the yard as Roxanne stood and

dusted off her knees. Throwing back her wide-brimmed hat, she started to speak, "How can I … Luke!"

"Hello, Roxanne." Luke smiled at her.

She smiled in return. "It's been a long time."

"I'd say." He nodded toward her outfit. "I've heard you've been busy."

"And happy," she said.

"I can see that. I'm happy for you. Loretta has some good news for you."

Her eyes widened. "The job? Really?"

"Go ask her yourself."

She threw her hat up in the air. "I will!" She started to run to the building and called back, "I'll be right back. Don't go anywhere!"

Luke chuckled. "Honey, I'm not going anywhere."

ACKNOWLEDGMENTS

Dear Reader,

There is no me, the author, without you, the reader. I value your precious resources and time. Thank you for spending time with Libby, Nick, Roxanne, and Luke today. I hope you relaxed and enjoyed a much deserved escape with a happily-ever-after ending.

If you enjoyed *Undisclosed*, will you consider writing a review and sharing it on Amazon, Bookbub, or Goodreads? Reviews help others decide if this book is right for them.

Special thanks to Peggy, Kelly Jo, Kimberly, and Jennifer for being advance readers of *Undisclosed*. And as always, thank you to my editor, Nicole.

If you have any feedback for me or would like to say hello, please email me at **elsa@elsamiles.com.**

I appreciate and value you.

Elsa